## Purchase Agreement
To get the home for your family

## Present Purchase Agreement
. Acceptance
. Rejection
. Counter Proposal

## Mortgage Application
. Credit Check Paid for in Advance
. Assets Verified
. Appraisal Paid for in Advance

## Home Inspection
## Homeowner Warranty
For Buyer's Protection

## Selection of Title Co.
## Title Search Performed
Protects Your Right of Ownership

## Mortgage Approval & Written Loan Commitment
Guarantees You Got The Loan

## Home Owners Insurance
Protects Your Investment
Be Careful of C.L.U.E.

## Termite Inspection
For Buyer Protection

## Transfer Utilities to Buyer's Name
To Save You Money

Tel. 202-997-0129 ❖ E-Mail info@legacyofpower.com ❖ Website: http://www.legacyofpower.com

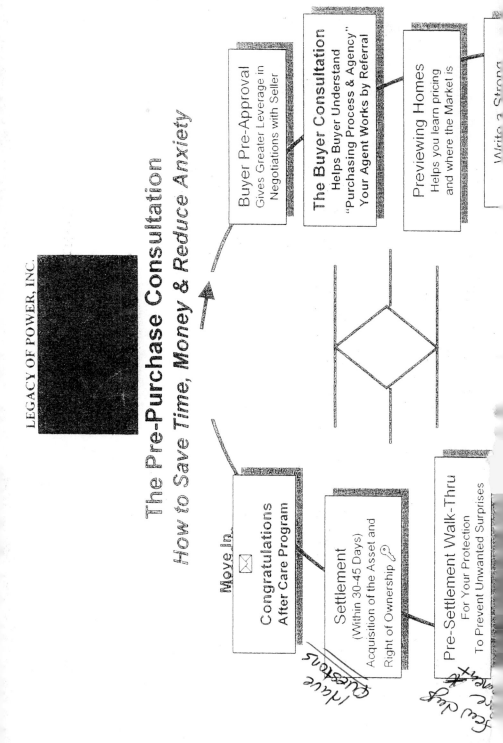

# A Mind To Build

What every new homebuyer should know
before they buy a home

Derick W. Hungerford

## Biblical Reference

• Unless otherwise noted, scripture references taken from the King James Version of the Bible.

• Scriptures taken from the Holy Bible, New International Version®, NIV®. Copyright © 1973, 1978, 1984 by Biblica, Inc™. Used by permission of Zondervan. All rights reserved worldwide. http://www.zondervan.com.

To ensure compliance with requirements imposed by the IRS, I inform you that any U.S. federal tax advice contained in this book is presented for informational purposes only and it not intended as a substitute for obtaining professional advice. This information cannot be used by any person for the purpose of (1) avoiding tax-related penalties or (2) recommending to another person any transaction or matter addressed in this book. I recommend that you consult with properly licensed legal, tax, and investment advisors for specific advice pertaining to your individual situation,

## Dedication

I dedicate this book to Leon F. Hunt who went home to the Lord in September 2010. Leon worked as a Mortgage Consultant for Residential Mortgage Corporation for 12 years. He was instrumental in presenting much of the information in this book for the weekly broadcast of the RMC Home and Wealth Show. For seven years Leon and I spent hours each week preparing and hosting the radio broadcast along with Cheryl Jackson. Leon gave of himself and never expected anything in return.

Leon, the RMC family will always remember your dedication, helpfulness, your baritone voice and your hearty appetite. .

## Acknowledgements

I first give honor and glory to my Lord and Savior, Jesus Christ; the author and finisher of my faith. I thank God for His grace and mercy and for the opportunity to share the information contained in this book. I would like to share my appreciation for my parents, George and Barbara Hungerford, your love and support has meant the world to me. I honor and love you both very much; I am so thankful that I've been blessed with such awesome parents. A special appreciation goes to my brother Darin Hungerford who is not only my sibling, but my friend, confidant, encourager, business partner and co-owner of Residential Mortgage Corporation. I could not have prayed for a better brother than you. We've been through so much in this industry, but having you with me has meant the world to me. Thank you brother... I love you. I thank my Pastor John Cherry II, Pastor of From the Heart Church Ministries®. My life has never been the same since joining in 1995 which interestingly enough was the same year and month Residential Mortgage Corporation was founded. Thank you Pastor Cherry for your boldness and example. I also acknowledge my executive assistant Angela Evans who has been my right hand person for the past 10 years. Thank you especially for your patience and for putting up with me. Through the ups and downs you were there...you are God sent. I recognize my dedicated support staff and friends:

Pleshette Johnson, Angelita Martin, Tesa Thompson, Carl Felton and all of RMC Mortgage Loan Consultants that have been a part of our Mortgage Firm. Thank you for your years of support; from the mountain top highs to the valley lows of the Mortgage Crisis of 2007, you all have remained dedicated, uplifting and encouraging. I especially thank you for our earlier daily prayers, which made us who we are. Thank you to our mortgage loan processing teams, you have made life easier through the constant changes in the mortgage industry. Gratitude goes to Chuck Ottley for your years of experience and willingness to always give a helping hand. I acknowledge the good people of Home Free USA, President and Founder, Marcia Griffin and Jim Griffin. Thank you for all that you do Milan Grifin; the excellent professional staff, Peyton Herbert, Barbara Hampton, Alfreda Williams, Gigi and Gary Plummer. You all are doing a wonderful work, thank you for your commitment to our community. I want to also thank my investment advisor and very good friend Glen Jackson for your constant encouragement, hours of conversation concerning money, finance and life, and your comical outlook in every situation (are you ever serious?). You have helped me in ways that you don't know. A thank you to James Diggs of UCAP, continue to do what you are doing; your labor is not in vain! Special acknowledgement to my good friend Cheryl Jackson (current Host of Praise 104.1 FM) who I co-hosted the RMC Home and Wealth show for 7 years on Heaven 1580 am. Myself, you and Leon had some great times in the studio, "those were the days". Keep "blessing" the people as you've done for years. I thank Nadine N. Amado who was the first person I sat down with to discuss this book. That day changed my life; I appreciate you and I thank you for being the faithful and virtuous woman of God that you are. You Nadine, are amazing! I appreciate all of my readers; some who put up with me for months talking about getting this book finished, Earnest Burley, Kirk Blackman, Patrice Psague, Dwayne Ellis, Nadine Amado, Perry Paylor, Brett Pulley, Emerick Peace, Cerissa M. O'Neal, Chuck Ottley, Glen Jackson and Neil Wright and Kathy Minus. And finally I would like to acknowledge all of my past and present clients for supporting our Mortgage Firm. You are the reason why we do what we do and we appreciate your patronage and support.

# Contents

## Recommendations

There are two ways to learn, from experience or from wisdom. When one learns from experience, one often suffers consequences that become "wisdom" for later choices. However when one learns from wisdom, they can avoid those costly consequences. In "A Mind to Build," Mr. Hungerford instructs the home buyer with simple to understand concepts that facilitate an action plan to "get it right the first time." Learning from Mr. Hungerford's wisdom recorded in this prolific publication will empower the home buyer before they take action that they might avoid common mistakes, think long-term, save dollars and avoid buyer's remorse, often caused by a lack of key information and strategies. This book is a must read for those who want no regrets.

Glen Jackson
Financial Advisor
*Capital Financial Group, H. Beck Inc.*

------------------------------------------------------------

In this great nation of ours, which promises all of us the rights to the America dream, there are two great tools that everyone who has achieved that to the fullest have used: business and home ownership. There are many resources that provide honest direction on how to own a business but for home ownership the limited resources available tend to be one dimensional at best and at worst misleading. In his latest book *A Mind to*

*Build,* successful entrepreneur and mortgage expert Derick Hungerford brings together his years of experience in helping thousands achieve the American dream of home ownership and his business acumen as a successful entrepreneur to provide us with a simple, yet honest, guide on how to own a our own home and keep it. I, for one, will take his advice. Thank you Derick for this timely and insightful resource."

> Patrice Tsague
> Chief Servant Officer
> Nehemiah Project International Ministries Inc.

----------------------------------------------------------------

"Finally, a smart, plain-spoken guide to home ownership has arrived. By sharing his insight, knowledge and wisdom in this book, Derick Hungerford has crafted a blue print for achieving what is still the quintessential American dream. If this book had been available 10 years ago, many Americans would have avoided becoming victims of the great mortgage meltdown. This is a most valuable tool for anyone who aspires to own a home. Let the real estate rebound begin!"

> Brett A. Pulley, dean of The Scripps Howard School of Journalism and Communications at Hampton University
> and author of "The Billion Dollar BET: Robert Johnson and the Inside Story of Black Entertainment Television

----------------------------------------------------------------

Derick cuts through the complexities of the home ownership process and helps the reader to navigate the mortgage finance maze in a way that allows them to fit the process to their own individual circumstances. The step-by-step approach of the book results in a usable, practical guide that he has wisely coupled with examples and encouragement so that the reader is able to make informed decisions.

Kirk Blackman
Financial Advisor
Blackman Financial Services

---------------------------------------------------------------

"For too many of us, there is a gap between what we do and what we dream of doing. Derick Hungerford has hit the nail squarely on the head with *A Mind To Build*, a step by step how to guide to successfully navigate the home buying process. He has expert industry knowledge and is uniquely equipped to advise anyone and assist with what should be everyone's goal of attaining homeownership."

- Neill S. Wright,
  CEO and president of First Tuskegee Bank

---------------------------------------------------------------

This is a great piece of informative work! Kudos to you for putting together such a useful and heartfelt product! I'm confident you readers will have a totally different mindset about renting versus owning and be properly educated and equipped to handle the process of home stewardship after reading you book.

I also loved the quotes. From page 22 with quotes surrounding how exactly wealthy people think opposite of poor people to page 19 with quotes explaining the mentality of achievers to page 14 where it is noted that you will be tomorrow where your thoughts take you to page 28 that so eloquently details how the fruit of our success is all about the root of our based on the seeds that we sow! The great quotes go on and on.

Keep up the impressive work and your diligence to educate people on the home buying process. I applaud your passion, your integrity, you knowledge, and your competence.

Erneŝt Burley
Burley and Associates Financial Services

------------------------------------------------------------

To all who have been Blessed to read this book:

You have in your hands a blueprint for success in your Home Ownership endeavors. Derick brings a wealth of talent as a tried and proven Mortgage Professional. Coming though the worst financial crisis in our lifetimes, Derick Hungerford and Residential Mortgage Corporation, the Company he shepherds, are still standing, but thriving and serving as a beacon of light, upholding the standards of God. Derick brings compassion in his approach to the Mortgage business, and the wisdom of almost 2 decades of transactional experience helping people successfully finance, and ultimately own their homes. "A Mind to Build" is a wonderful insight into the proper process and marvelous mindset needed for fulfilling home buying experience. Probably the greatest attribute of The Author, and the Book, is the fact that both are God directed, God inspired, rooted, grounded and dependent on the Word of God, and the Truth.

I believe that a well prepared home Buyer, with proper expectation, and accurate information, will do very well in any market. I believe that reading this book will accomplish that for you. Read, underline, highlight, re-read, take notes, apply the knowledge and then enjoy the home buying experience that you will now be well prepared for.

Realtors, like myself can help you find the right home, but then begins to duty to repay that mortgage. Therefore, it is important that you follow Proverbs 4:7 as it states; Wisdom is the principal thing; therefore get wisdom: and with thy getting get understanding.

Enjoy, learn, apply, and prosper, in Jesus name Amen

Chuck Ottley
Broker, Dominion Sellstate Realty

-----------------------------------------------------------

"*A Mind to Build* is not just a real estate book for first-time homebuyers; it's a book about life skills, stewardship and wealth building. *A Mind to Build* is a must read for anyone wanting to get their financial house in order and keep it that way!"

~ Cerissa M. O'Neal, Esq.,
Managing Member of Milestone Title, LLC

-----------------------------------------------------------

This book was far overdue. The author delivers a clear and succinct path to home ownership and more importantly consumer/client education. This is an absolute read for anyone considering to buy or anyone looking to gain more knowledge of the real estate/mortgage industry.   This is a truly professional guide to build your mind.

Emerick A.  Peace
Real Estate Consultant
Keller Williams Realty

# A Mind to Build

**Derick W. Hungerford**
derick@amindtobuild.com
dhungerford@myrmcloan.com

Visit Us TODAY!
http://www.amindtobuild.com
&
http://www.myrmcloan.com

301-773-9811

*And God is able to make all grace abound toward you; that ye always having all sufficiency in all things, may abound to every good work.*

**2 Corinthians 8**

## Preface

Today's Homebuyers need a lift and an easier pathway to success. Buying a home is no joke and for those of you who intend to move, want more room and are just sick and tired of living where you are now.... reading "A Mind to Build" is a great start.

Derick Hungerford is a great teacher and an excellent mortgage professional. He is knowledgeable, personable, caring, and honest. Whether in his homebuying class or in his office for a pre approval, you can count on him to protect your interest and reinforce what you need to know to get the best deal possible.

The mortgage industry pushes renting as a way to stabilize America. Derick pushes homeownership as a way to stabilize you. Don't be misled.

92% of all homeowners served by my organization HomeFree~USA, wished that they'd become more informed before buying their homes. Having someone to simplify the process, be honest about the pro's and con's of various mortgage products and tell you the industry pitfalls- is what all homebuyers need and few homeowners got when buying their homes.

If you haven't taken one of Derick's classes ~you should. He is an excellent teacher who can break things down so even the uninterested will be interested. He's good and he is resourceful.

As we progress in life, we have to ask ourselves: what am I accomplishing? How am I progressing? When many of us look at our financial accomplishments, we see an apartment that's too small; furniture that we're still paying for; a neighborhood that you want to change; bills that you want to pay down; a credit score that you want to improve and a sense of independence that seems elusive as the years go by. Don't let these things get you down; your best days are ahead of you. Homeownership will bring you joy and a sense of achievement; it may take some time to get there but you will.

Move forward in finances and in homeownership with Derick Hungerford by your side. His words of wisdom are proven, his knowledge expert and his sincerity guaranteed. "A Mind to Build" may just be what you need to carry you home. HomeFree~USA and our homebuyers love Derick and this book. You will too.

Enjoy.

Marcia Griffin
President~ HomeFree~USA

## Introduction:

*If a man writes a book, let him set down only what he knows. I have guesses enough of my own.*

Johann Wolfgang Von Goethe
German Poet, Novelist, and Philosopher

I hope that this book will help and guide you through your journey to achieve home ownership. I am delighted to share *A Mind to Build* with you. As you read, you will inevitably build upon your dreams, aspirations, and your individual goal to be a homeowner one page at a time. Having the right mindset will be important as you approach your goal. For some, a complete paradigm shift is imperative to have a successful and fulfilling journey. I hope this book will inspire you to move with confidence, peace, and clarity through the home-buying process.

I have been blessed to serve thousands of homebuyers over the years and have received tons of questions and requests for guidance. The information and examples in this book are compiled from my seventeen years of experience and research. I have also had the privilege of hosting the *RMC Home and Wealth Radio Show* on Heaven 1580 AM in the Washington, DC, area. Much of the information you will read in this book is a result of researching and organizing topics for that weekly radio show.

I believe that home ownership is a very important aspect of our financial lives, and buying a home has proven to be a very good financial decision. However, I often advise my clients that a mortgage can be a double-edged sword. In other words, for some, buying a home has been one of the best decisions they have ever made. Purchasing has offered all of the benefits and blessings that you will read about in this book. Home ownership has improved their financial life, family life, and net worth. Buying a home has essentially given them a raise in their income through various tax laws and has given the homeowner an opportunity to bless generations to come.

On the other hand, for some, buying a home has been a source of heartache and financial decline. Unfortunately, I have seen many homeowners get hurt financially due to market swings and bad decisions. I honestly think that if some of these homeowners would have been privy to the information in this book, their situation would be different. Years ago, the adage in the real estate market was *location, location, location*. Things have changed since the housing market collapsed in 2007. The three most important words today are *education, education, education*!

I have had the fortunate opportunity to study a vast amount of homebuyers' journeys through the buying process. Some handled the process with perseverance and grace. Others lost their peace and even their character. The difference between the two is the home buyer's approach and mindset. This book will at times focus on the *mindset* of buying a home, which I believe is just as important as simply learning the steps of buying a home. I also believe that success happens twice; it happens first in the mind, and then those thoughts are manifested on the outside. Thus it is critically important to start the home-buying process with the proper mindset. The purchase process must start with *a mind to build*.

# Chapter 1

## Breaking Ground

Before any building project gets under way or breaks ground, there must be a vision, a plan, and a blueprint. The person who has the vision may not necessarily know how to build. However, that does not stop the project from getting started. Traditional building projects require teams of developers, construction companies, plumbers, electricians, interior-design workers, and more. Similarly, you will need professionals to help you bring your plan to fruition. These professionals include your mortgage banker, realtor, tax planner, investment advisor, and insurance agent. It will be wise to surround yourself with a team of professional advisors who will be able to help you during *and* after you purchase your new home.

Consider this book to be a member of that team. As you read you will see that we are laying the foundation and building on your dream, your family's legacy, your wealth, your security, or your lifestyle change. Whatever it may be, you are beginning a process of building. I know you are excited about the possibility of owning a new home. I want to congratulate you for deciding to take this monumental step toward making it a reality. Many first-time buyers have walked this path before you, and millions more will do the same long after your purchase is final. Think about it: sooner than you know, you will receive your keys and make your new house your home.

Home ownership provides a broad range of benefits that are shared by individuals and society—and to the economy as it relates to stimulating its growth and expansion. Owning a home is a long-term investment that can create incredible financial freedom. Planned correctly and used wisely, this freedom can and will have a great impact not only on your children but also on your children's children. The first step in becoming a homeowner is ensuring you are mentally and spiritually prepared for the task at hand.

During the home-buying process, some people experience reservations, inhibitions, and anxiety, but I encourage you not to lose your faith. "And let us not be weary in well doing: for in due season we shall reap, if we faint not" (Galatians 6:9). If you are willing to get focused and be committed, your journey toward home ownership can be a very enjoyable experience. Anxiousness breeds anxiety, which can lead to discouragement, discontent, and distraction during this process. So patience, prayer, and perseverance will be your guide. "Be anxious for nothing, but in everything by prayer and supplication, with thanksgiving, let your requests be made known to God" (Philippians 4:6).

Before seeking home ownership, you must decide whether you are ready. I know this is probably a simple question, but it important that you determine if this is truly where you want to be. So take a minute to ask yourself the following questions: "Am I ready to start moving toward making this huge change in my life?" "Am I prepared to see this endeavor to the end?" If your answer is yes to both, then you have made a wise decision.

By deciding that you are ready, you are making one of the most important investments you will ever make. And you are accepting the responsibility of doing something that will pay dividends for a lifetime. You should be commended!

It is important to identify and understand the *whys* behind your *wise* decision. I often ask first-time homebuyers, "Why are you buying a home?" You see, the more *valid* reasons you can identify, the more firm your foundation, which is extremely important in this sometimes-challenging pursuit. Anthony Robbins put it like this, "if you can find enough reasons to do anything, something inside of you will find a way to accomplish that goal."

Now that you have determined that you are ready to change your circumstance and know why you made that determination, you can now consider other factors that may not be as significant as the purchase itself but may have an impact when you are actually able to pursue your goal. Ask yourself these questions: "Am I ready to cut my own lawn?" "What happens if the water heater breaks and has to be replaced within the first year?" "Do I have reserve funds for improvements to my home?" Reserve capital and home maintenance are real factors and can have a tremendous impact on your success in home owning and are sometimes lost in the excitement of making a choice to buy a home.

There are numerous pros and cons for owning your own home, but the benefits will always outweigh the downside if you are prepared. As a new homeowner, you should always be prepared; having a plan is paramount. Things do not always go as planned. Appliances break, faucets leak—life happens; knowing that you will be carrying the load of responsibility for these possible setbacks is a decision that must be understood. Your commitment to preparedness for the unknown must not waiver.

Owning a home can result in building wealth over time. For example, if you were to pay $1,200 each month in rent for thirty years, with modest increases over that time period, you will have paid your landlord over one-half million dollars in rent. That is an incredible number! What will you have to show for the $532,080 you will have paid toward housing? Absolutely nothing! Can you start to visualize how many people have nothing to show for a lifetime of making rental payments? Unfortunately many of these families will stay in the perpetual cycle of rent bondage forever.

Many people mistakenly believe renting is cheaper than owning a home; actually, owning a home can be cheaper. Under certain circumstances when real estate values are overpriced and rents are low, there may be some short-term advantages to renting. However, renting simply is not a good deal (except for the landlord). As discussed previously, if you do not own your home, you can easily wind up spending one-half million dollars on rent during the course of a lifetime. If the landlord increases the rent by 5 percent per year, you will pay about $1 million over the same period. At the end, you'll have nothing to show other than a stack of canceled checks.

**Equity**

If you were to invest in a $200,000 home and pay down on the mortgage for thirty years (assuming appreciation at a rate of 6 percent), you would be left owning a home worth approximately $1.1 million. In addition if you buy a home and pay $1,200 to $1,500 a month, the monthly payments will be fixed (no increasing payments like rent). In this scenario, the only thing that will increase is the value of the home (please note property taxes have a tendency to increase and decrease as well). The real upside with equity appreciation is you do not have to split the profits with the lender. The entire profit belongs to you! This is what is called a lifestyle change; a way to stop living with worries of where you are going to live down the road or how you'll be able to leave a legacy for your family.

Along with financial freedom, you will have the freedom of having your own place, with your own rules (for some not necessarily the best thing), and the ability to do whatever you choose—within limits of local, state, and federal laws, of course. Knowing you can knock down any wall, repaint, add a gym, put in a hot tub, or build a deck can be very satisfying. The freedom to make these types of changes is normally prohibited when renting.

Home ownership turns homeowners into savers, and that plays a big part in becoming financially successful. In general people who have money have it because they saved it. Whereas people who do not have money did not save. Each time you make a mortgage payment, you are essentially saving money.

There are two ways for your homes equity to grow (1) paying down of the mortgage balance and (2) the effects of normal appreciation. The longer you own your home, the more equity you build, and the more money you save, the more financially fit you will become.

**Tax Advantage**

There are also tax breaks for homeowners. You will be able deduct real estate taxes and interest paid on your first home, which is a huge savings. Current tax laws also allow deductions for energy savings, improvements, and certain appliances.

The best way to stay poor is to pay more than you have to in taxes. As a renter, that's just what you are doing. When you rent, you get absolutely zero tax breaks on your housing costs. As a homeowner you get lots of breaks. One of the best tax breaks that homeowners enjoy is the mortgage interest deduction. When you own a home, the IRS allows you to deduct from your taxable income the interest charges you pay on the first $1 million of your home mortgage—which means that if your mortgage is $1 million or less, you get to deduct all your interest payments. Because for the first ten years of a standard thirty-year mortgage, nearly 80 percent of your monthly payment goes to pay off interest charges, you can write off more than three-quarters of what you pay in mortgage payments. You will also be able to write off 100 percent of your property taxes as well. The point is that those tax deductions you get to take for mortgage interest are a *gift* from the government—take the gift.

Another way to stay poor is to keep letting Uncle Sam take a good portion of the profits you make from your investment. If you buy shares of stock for $300 and sell them for $600, you would probably conclude that you have doubled your money. This kind of profit is called capital gains, and as with just about all other income, Uncle Sam wants his cut, of course. If the stock was held for twelve months or less, you would pay taxes based on the normal tax bracket (depending on your tax bracket—in this example approximately $80 in taxes). If it has been held for longer than twelve months, this would be considered long-term capital gains tax and would be assessed at 15 percent. For the homeowner who bought the $200,000 home that appreciated 10 percent per year for five years, they can now sell their home for $351,000 for a profit of $151,000—*tax free.* (If it were taxed normally, Uncle Sam would have taken over $30,000 of *your* money.) If you are renting but want to improve your financial condition, nothing that you will ever do in your lifetime is likely to make you as much money as buying a primary, owner-occupied home. Remember, when you buy a home, you are doing more than just buying a place to live. If done properly, home ownership can be a foundation on which you can build wealth, even if you never earn more than you are earning right now.

## Leverage

Living in your home and paying down your mortgage does two things: it allows you to build equity and to use *other people's money* (OPM), which is another term for leverage. In other words, using OPM may be one of the best tools for creating wealth. Paying down your mortgage allows you to save a considerable amount of interest over time as you pay your mortgage back with cheaper dollars as a result of inflation. This can and will add up to thousands of dollars over the life of your loan. Leverage is one of the three financial miracles that I teach in our home-buying seminars. Buying properties with OPM gives you huge financial advantages and allows you to multiply your gains. The *other* people in this case will be your mortgage company.

For example, let's say you found a home for $200,000 and you qualify for the USDA 100 percent loan. This means the balance on your home will be $200,000. Now let's say the value of the house goes up by 10 percent per year—after the first year, your property value would be "worth" $220,000, an increased profit of $20,000 in one year. If you were to sell your home after the first year, you would make $20,000 and the bank or the mortgage company does not share in the profits from the sale. Your rate of return is infinite because you did not make a down payment! As much as I believe in diversifying your financial portfolio, there is little chance any other investment will produce anything close to this kind of return. There is also no chance that anyone will lend you 100 percent of the purchase price to buy stock, bonds, or mutual funds. Such investments require you to use your own money. In the case of buying a home, you are using someone else's money to benefit yourself!

Leverage allows you not only to own and live in your home but also allows you to have investment opportunities and use the equity in your home to purchase additional homes for rentals or vacations. Leverage and equity are two aspects of buying real estate that can lead to wealth! Now that we have briefly discussed the pros and cons of buying, let's start the work. It is time to develop, *a mind to build.*

# Chapter 2

*For as he thinketh in his heart, so is he*
*Proverbs 23:7*

## Changing Your Mindset

Now that you have determined home ownership may be right for you, it is imperative to make sure you change the way you think about money, mortgage, and finance. Financial success starts in the mind and will eventually become evident as you start to implement those successful thoughts. You will need to first decide what you want. Next, you have to believe what you want is possible. Then, you must focus on it by thinking about it and visualizing it as if it were already yours. Finally, you must be willing to pay the price to get it with hard work, discipline, effort, and perseverance. The success or failure of your journey of home ownership will depend on your mindset.

## The Four Enemies of Life

One of my business coaches taught me that there are four enemies of life that are responsible for destroying the lives and dreams of countless people. I have related these enemies to buying a home, and I often present them to my first-time homebuyers in hopes of identifying potential roadblocks. In order to be the successful homeowner that I am sure you aspire to be, you will have to first become that person right now. Let's look at these four enemies of life to see if you can identify with any of them. Let's work together to remedy the challenges you face so that nothing stands between you and the fulfillment of your destiny.

## Fear

It has been said that FEAR stands for False Evidence Appearing Real. The reality is that fear is a real emotion usually birthed from what we see, hear, or feel. Fear usually leads to feelings of anxiety, agitation, and doubt. Now imagine going through the process of buying a home with these unhealthy feelings. Fear also plays on our imagination and has caused many to be paralyzed. Fear takes your focus off of what you know and puts it on something you see, hear, or feel. *Fear and faith can't operate together.* If you cannot find a way to rid your mind of fear, all of your actions and reactions during your home-buying process will be based on fear.

Confidence is a trait that can be developed and strengthened every day. During the home-buying process, you will be challenged by fear, worry, and uncertainty. If you let it, fear can be a constant mental struggle that you must overcome if you are going to be successful.

The following passage was written by Marianne Williamson in her book *A Return to Love:*

*Our deepest fear is not that we are inadequate. Our deepest fear is that we are powerful beyond measure. It is our light, not our darkness that frightens us. We ask ourselves, who am I to be brilliant, gorgeous, talented and fabulous? Actually, who are we not to be? You are a child of God. Your playing small doesn't serve the world.*

*There's nothing enlightened about shrinking so that other people won't feel insecure around you. We were born to make manifest the glory of God that is within us. It's not just in some of us, it's in everyone. And as we let our own light shine, we unconsciously give other people permission to do the same. As we are liberated from our own fears, our presence automatically liberates others.*

## Confusion

Lack of clarity produces confusion, and conflicting thoughts or opinions feed that confusion. If you shape your thoughts, your vision will focus, and clarity will appear. Cluttered thinking will always leave you bewildered. The Bible says that a double-minded man is unstable in all of his ways. Your thought patterns are a direct link to your outcome. Educating yourself will help you. Thomas Jefferson once said, "Knowledge is light, the more you acquire the brighter it becomes." Challenge your confusion through education (like reading this book), and I guarantee that clarity will result.

## Doubt

Each time you doubt yourself, you lose a little bit of your confidence. Being positive and confident during this process is a must. Buying a home is a big deal, and everyone won't have the opportunity to live that dream. Many of us have beliefs that limit our success—whether they're beliefs about our own capabilities, beliefs about what it takes to finance a home loan, beliefs on getting a "good deal," or even prior beliefs or myths from our parents or grandparents that have long since been refuted. Moving beyond your limiting beliefs—and your doubts—are critical first steps toward becoming a successful homeowner.

During this process I hope you will constantly renew your mind to erase those doubts!

## Disorganization

In my local church, we are taught that organization is God's plan to simply your life. During the initial meeting with clients, I can sense right away whether I am dealing with an organized person or an unorganized person. As you'll learn later, there are certain items that are required to be presented at the initial application. I've had times when clients could only find one or two out of the six items requested...*un*organized. At the other (disorganized) extreme, I had one time when the borrower brought far more than necessary to the meeting. I went back to my personal office while the client got situated in the conference room. To my total surprise, when I got back to the conference room, the conference table was completely filled with papers, documents, envelopes, booklets, etc. Think about this: all unorganized people are a little dysfunctional, and they punish all the other people in their lives. A person's desk and car are microcosms of their lives. Looking at both can reveal a lot about a person. Add the checkbook, and that person's life story becomes an open book. Organization is a key ingredient to a successful home-buying process.

## The Mindset

A renter's mindset is completely different from a homeowner's mindset. As a renter, you depend largely on your landlord to take responsibility for that property. Your personal stewardship for that property is limited to paying your rent (on time) and reporting when repairs need to be completed. As a homeowner, the responsibilities are all yours. You are the sole steward and will be responsible for everything that happens, good or bad, within the four walls of the home.

I often compare buying a home to owning your own business. *Your home is your business*, and you'll need to understand business practices in order to run your home efficiently and effectively. Similarly, employees have a different mindset than employers or business owners. As a renter, you essentially are a worker for your landlord. It is my hope and desire for you now to become your own landlord and get into the business of running your own company The benefits are far reaching.

Although home ownership may not be for everyone, I believe that for some, renting can lead to an impoverished mindset and can cause us to live beneath our potential. There is no reason for us to think that we should be content, satisfied, or comfortable with working to make other people (landlords) rich. Every time we pay our rent, the owner of the property gets the benefit. Being satisfied to have a roof over our heads (rental unit) is wonderful, but when being satisfied starts to breed complacency, we have the responsibility of changing our minds.

Changing our minds means that we have decided against a previous thought and are now leaning toward a contrary decision. Once we change our minds, what once was comfortable will become uncomfortable. What used to be acceptable is now unacceptable. This must happen in order for us to develop a mind to build. From proper savings patterns to intelligent spending habits, we must start anew with a mind to build.

Having a mind to build is the initial stage (the foundation) of home ownership. The difference between being a tenant to being a homeowner is so much more than "ownership." This monumental step can possibly be a blessing not only to you but possibly to your children and their children.

Many people are unaware of the advantages of home ownership. In most cases I have found that renters don't believe they can afford the responsibility of a mortgage; however, the fact that they are maintaining a lease agreement contradicts this mindset.

If you can afford to pay $1,200 per month to rent an apartment, you can certainly afford to pay a mortgage in the same price range. How does this work, you ask? Well, home ownership allows you to carry certain tax benefits (which we will cover in detail later), which can allow you to see more of your money. As a result, you literally give yourself a pay increase simply by purchasing a home.

Living as a tenant can be very comfortable, but it can also prevent you from taking control of your life and becoming independent. Renting may give us a sense of home, but in reality it doesn't belong to us. A few of the benefits of renting are that there is only a security deposit needed, the landlord is responsible for repairs and maintenance, porter service is provided for the property, and you have access to property recreation such as a pool and a clubhouse. Some of the disadvantages include not having special financial benefits such as tax deductions and not sharing in the appreciation value, being subject to small (or no) grace periods for payments, and limited parking space for guests.

There is a difference between being comfortable and being complacent. When we become so comfortable depending on a landlord to provide a living space and willing to adhere to a list of rules in order to continue to occupy the apartment, we run the risk of being complacent. As crazy as it may sound, the reality is that renting can become addictive.

*You are today where your thoughts have brought you; you will be tomorrow where your thoughts take you.*
James Allen
Author

While your apartment home continues to appreciate in value, the only increase you experience as a tenant is in your monthly payments every year. If the landlord is experiencing profits on the property appreciation, why is there a need to raise your monthly payments?

The answer is quite simple. Leaseholders are a major part of the investment or vested interest in what will ultimately make the landlord wealthy.

If you are going to buy or build the home of your dreams, you are going to have to make the commitment and stick to it. This commitment may take time and sacrifice. As my pastor has said, "Life requires sacrifice, it is not an option. You'll either sacrifice now, or you will sacrifice later...either way, you will sacrifice." With proper discipline you can begin to see yourself financially capable and living in your own home. As I discussed earlier, before any building is erected or construction gets under way, the commitment starts in the mind. If we are going to make the transition from tenant to owner, we first have to make the transition in our minds.

*Ninety-nine percent of all failures come from people who have a habit of making excuses.*
George Washington Carver

## The Dangers of Entitlement Theory

Changing your mindset sometimes can be a difficult and daunting task. It will determine if you are a successful homebuyer or not. One of the most pervasive myths in American culture today is that we are entitled to a great life; that somehow, somewhere, someone (certainly not us) is responsible for filling our lives with continual happiness, great investments, the home of our dreams, and an exciting career simply because we exist.

On the contrary, we must take 100 percent responsibility for everything that we experience in life. This includes the level of our achievements, the results of our mortgage approval, our financial status, etc. Many people have been conditioned to blame something outside of themselves for the parts of their life that are not going well. If you want to create the results that you desire while seeking to purchase your home, you will need to take 100 percent responsibility for your current status and future results. That means giving up all of the excuses, all the victim stories, all the reasons why you can't and why you have not, and all of the blaming of outside circumstances.

The market in which you decide to purchase will give you an indication of the mindset that should be employed. Sometimes homebuyers aren't willing to change, and it can cause them to sit on the sidelines of despair as their counterparts eagerly and aggressively put down contract offers on available properties. For example, as I am writing this book, although we have a long way to go, the market may be slowly turning. However, there are still many homes on the market (a lot due to foreclosure). Homebuyers have begun to catch on that *now* is the time to buy.

## One Way to Approach the Home-Buying Process

*The man who complains about the way the ball bounces is likely the one who dropped it.*
Lou Holtz, NCAA Coach

Because of all the talk about a buyer's market, one of my clients (I'll call him Mr. Barksdale) *refuses* to change his mindset. Although I and his realtor have repeatedly educated him on the importance of offering a fair price on a good property, Mr. Barksdale continues to think that he can have his cake and eat it too. In a recent conversation, he had an opportunity to make an offer on a home that had several other offers pending. Instead of giving an honest and best offer, his mindset was to offer a low price and ask for the maximum closing help. Although he understood that the competition was stiff, he convinced himself that he *deserved* it all—a low payment, a low price, all closing paid, an ideal location, and not use *any* of his own money on the purchase. By the way, this was the third property that Mr. Barksdale had made an offer on; the other two were rejected. Because of his entitlement mentality, he has and will continue to hold his family back from getting ahead financially. Instead of focusing on the purpose of buying a home, Mr. Barksdale would rather focus on what he can get right now. He *thinks* that he can continue to hold on to the same mindset and have different results. As you may have heard, continuing to do the same things over and over again while expecting different results is the definition of insanity. The thought that the homebuyer is entitled to have it all and not be affected by the current market is a very dangerous and unfounded way of thinking.

Unfortunately, Mr. Barksdale's current mindset will cause him and his family to live beneath their potential. I explained to him that he must sacrifice something in order to get something better; however, it fell on deaf ears. His current way of thinking says, "I would rather not offer a fair price and keep my family in a rental home while wasting hundreds of thousands of dollars in rent." He had been renting for approximately thirty-four years. His current rent payment is $1,100 (by the way, he indicated that he did not want to pay more than $900 for a mortgage). Using an average rent payment of $700, he has paid over $285,000 over the last thirty-four years. Needless to say, Mr. Barksdale never purchased a home and is currently renting, now for more than thirty-five years.

### A Better Approach to the Home-Buying Process

Let's now compare the example to another client, Ms. Osbourne. I asked her some very important questions:

Are you able to afford a home?
Her answer: Yes.
Why do you want to buy a home?
Her answer: Tax benefits and investment opportunities.
Are you willing to do whatever it takes?
Her answer: Yes I am.

She went on to say that although she was attempting to use a down-payment-assistance program, she was willing to use her money if needed. She said that she would cut back on her spending and put an additional $300 in her savings account monthly. She also agreed to stop using her ATM card and would give herself a minimum amount for an allowance. She said she would offer fair pricing and would be committed to the process. Although Ms. Osbourne wanted to get her entire closing costs paid by the seller, she looked at each offer circumstance differently. Her focus was to offer a fair price and ask for closing help. She understood that there would be a sacrifice and realized that there was a possibility that she would not be able to get everything she wanted in the home of her choice. She was able to differentiate between her *must have's* and *would like to have's*. When updated documents were needed, she e-mailed them right away because she always saved electronic versions. She knew what she wanted to pay on a monthly basis but realized that the payment could fluctuate a little based on the property tax amount for each home. Ms. Osbourne had a completely different outlook than Mr. Barksdale. She was prepared to sacrifice in order to get to the finish line.

She is currently in her single-family home enjoying life.

**Doing Your Best Is Not Good Enough!**

I know this may not sound encouraging, but it is the truth. It's a good chance that you have already done your best. And your best has gotten you to this point right now. If that is the case, then it's time to really make the sacrifices in order to get to the next level of your financial life. Since you've probably already done your best, let's take the next step...***Its time to do whatever it takes!*** You see, there is a big difference between achievers and dreamers. Many things are typically required to reach a successful outcome; however, the willingness to do whatever it takes adds an extra dimension to the desired goal that helps you persevere in the face of overwhelming challenges, setbacks, credit challenges, lack of resources, etc.

My question to you is: Are you willing to do whatever it takes to achieve your dream of home ownership? I often ask this question, and many homebuyers give me a resounding YES. And then I start talking about cutting the budget by staying out of certain stores, reducing coffee purchases, taking their lunch to work, or getting their hair done less frequently. And then the looks change and the enthusiasm subsides. The transformation during the conversation is comical sometimes. You may be experiencing it while you're reading right now.

Of course, if you don't know what the price is, you can't choose to pay it. Sometimes the first step is to investigate what will be required to achieve your goal. Only you can decide if buying a home is right for you and what price you are willing to pay. It may be that buying a home doesn't serve you in the long run. But if it does, find out what you need to do, and then set about doing it with all of your energy.

Unfortunately many home seekers have embraced the notion that they do not have to sacrifice. As quoted by Episcopal Pastor John A. Cherry, ***"Where there is no sacrifice, there is no appreciation"***.

Achievers determine the necessary sacrifice and then choose to make that sacrifice. A fine line separates achievers from dreamers. You may think talent, titles, or resources separate achievers from dreamers. However, if you spend some time with people who win, the line that splits these two groups of people becomes clear. The thing that separates these two groups is attitude. Achievers are dedicated to success no matter the obstacle. Achievers act despite circumstances, and they are willing to put forth the effort and pay the price of success.

Achievers don't make excuses, and they certainly don't play the blame game. Achievers take responsibility for the future, whereas dreamers blame circumstances or other people when facing a roadblock. Rather than wallowing in helplessness, achievers search diligently to overcome the obstacles in front of them. Achievers abstain from complaining. They recognize its weakness and guard their minds and mouths against indulging in this time-wasting activity. As George Washington Carver said, "ninety-nine percent of failures come from people who have a habit of making excuses."

I believe that we are where we are today because of the choices we made yesterday. I also believe that today we all are exactly where we want to be because *the essence of who we are is what we do, not what we say.*

Okay, it's now time for a gut check. Honestly, are you serious about purchasing a home? If the answer to this question is yes, then it's time to get serious, make no excuses, be courageous, and do *whatever it takes*!

### What Is Your Financial Blueprint?

It will be good for you to learn about your attitude toward credit, spending, and finances. I can spend five minutes with anyone and pretty much tell you their financial paradigm. Most people have one of three major financial paradigms—spender, saver, or producer. Many of us may have some combination of all three; however, most of us have one dominant blueprint personality.

*If I gave you $10,000 in cash right now, what would you do with it?*

Depending on your answer, you will fit in one of these three major financial paradigms. If you thought you would get furniture for your new home, you are a spender. If you thought you would pay off some debts or "I'll put it away for a rainy day," you are a saver. If you thought you would invest it to make more money (such as buying a home), you are a producer. The goal is to build a producer mindset.

## Spenders

Spenders make up 60 percent of the population. The main focus of spenders is to buy things. They make decisions based on scarcity, which says "If I don't buy this thing today, it won't be available in the future." Or, as one of my close friends always says, "But it's on sale!" My standard reply is, "The real sale is if you don't buy it at all."

Spenders simply feel that money is to be used to spend and not to keep. If they come into a large amount of money, they find a way to spend it. In my seminars I often ask my audience, "if I gave you $10,000 right now, what would you do with it?" Invariably I'll get a few who will say, "buy a car" or "get furniture." Spenders don't simply spend money; they "blow" money. Have you ever heard the statement, "that money is already spent"? My question becomes, how can you spend money that you don't have?

If you are a spender, it is imperative that you change your mindset when entering the home-buying market. Unfortunately, many people aren't able to handle money because they don't have the internal capability. It's all about what is inside that will eventually manifest itself on the outside. For example, nearly 90 percent of all lottery winners end up at their original financial level. They could not handle their newfound wealth. It was short-lived because they never changed their internal financial blueprint and ended up wasting their winnings.

**Savers**

Savers represent about 34 percent of the population. Their main focus is to pay off debt or save their money behind the bars of a financial institution. They frequently say they are saving for a rainy day. A saver would not dare use the $10,000 to buy things. While this is a better blueprint personality to have, both savers and spenders are being motivated by the same factors: fear and scarcity. Spenders operate under the assumption that, "if I don't buy it now, it won't be there for me later"—scarcity. A savers rational is, "I must save this money because something may happen and I must have enough money"—fear.

Having a scarcity mindset is based on fear. I often ask, "who in this seminar is motivated by security?" Almost all hands go up. Then I ask, "who in here is motivated by fear?" Again, almost all hands go up. This is because security and fear are both based on the same mindset—scarcity.

**Producers**

Investors make up about 6 percent of the population. They view the world in a more aggressive, positive, and confident way. They get excited about their $10,000 because they can see a thousand ways to make it earn even more money.

Someone with an investor blueprint understands that it has nothing to do with ownership and everything to do with control. For an investor it's about stewardship—meaning how much property he or she can take responsibility over with the least amount of money out of his or her pocket on a monthly basis. Investors are not really excited about having a payment either, but they go about doing things differently to eliminate as much of the payment as possible. This is exactly what home stewardship is about. When you purchase a home, you are taking control of a large possession. Producers understand that a home is virtually the only investment where they can earn a great return, enjoy tax-free profits, have control, use OPM to pay for it, and actually live in it. Wow! What other investment has all of those benefits?

## Totally Different Thinking

Have you ever noticed that wealthy people don't simply think differently from poor people, they think the total opposite? I borrowed these contradictory mindset examples from T. Harv Eker.

- ✓ Wealthy people have a lot of money and spend little.
  Poor people have little money and spend a lot.
- ✓ Wealthy people work to earn money for their investments.
  Poor people work to earn money to live today.
- ✓ Wealthy people buy assets.
  Poor people buy expenses.
- ✓ Wealthy people collect land.
  Poor people collect bills.
- ✓ Wealthy people constantly learn and grow.
  Poor people think they already know. (about money and finances)

Isn't that interesting? The thought patterns are the complete opposite between those who have money and those who don't.

Certain principles have been put on earth regarding money, and they will work for whoever uses them. When it rains, it rains on the just and the unjust alike. The better you manage your money, the more money you will probably acquire. Conversely, if you don't manage your money properly, the funds that you do have will never be enough. Although God has placed within every one of us the ability to take control of our financial circumstances, many will live their lives being controlled by the spirit of poverty. Their financial thermostat (mindset) has been programmed in such a way that they will be kept in financial bondage. The good news however, is that you can change your financial thermostat by changing your mindset, as simple as that.

Once you have successfully changed your mindset, we can focus our attention on the building project itself. Let's start to build the home of your dreams by first understanding the difference between ownership and stewardship. Understanding the difference is vital to your successful journey.

# Chapter 3

*For we brought nothing into this world, and it is certain we can carry nothing out.*
*I Timothy 6:7*

## Ownership versus Stewardship

We've talked a little about mindset as it pertains to buying a home. One important concept that is important to understand is that we as consumers can never own anything. Everything that we have belongs to the Lord...everything. For that reason you'll find from here on out, instead of using the words *home ownership*, I've termed owning a home as *home stewardship*. You see, when you think of *stewardship*, there is an entirely new thought pattern given to the item in question.

There is a big difference between being an owner of something and being a steward *over* something. Ownership will cause a person to believe that their home or property really does belong to them. When many people speak about ownership, the feeling one would get is that they can do whatever they want with it. This can be a short sighted and fundamentally self centered way of thinking. Ownership focuses on rights without the responsibilities.

However, *stewardship* denotes that you are being entrusted and indicates having more of a responsibility. Actually, everything is a gift and loan from God to be used wisely. That's exactly what buying a home is about. We are simply stewards over what was entrusted to us. Stewards are accountable to the Lord rather than to themselves. Although stewards recognize their right to do with their property whatever they want, they also recognize that with that right comes responsibility. Stewards treat everything as a loan, and they always understand the blessing behind it.

I have heard homeowners talk about working extremely hard to pay their mortgage off as soon as possible, so they will be able to say that they "own" their home. They like the feeling of saying their home is paid off, which by the way is a worthy goal. However, even if you did manage to pay your mortgage off, you will still have taxes, maintenance, and other upkeep responsibilities. At the very least, you will still have the liability of responsibility. Thus, you never own your home anyway. In other words, it's completely impossible to ever rid our lives of all the liabilities, so the concept of ownership is a fruitless quest. Stewards understand that nothing belongs to them even if they have it paid for and don't have a lien or a loan against it.

A steward's thinking says, "I am a grateful recipient of God's blessings, and I want to give it to him because I understand that I am a steward."

God has given us stewardship over all that He has brought into our lives—our abilities, our gifts, our income, and our increase. He brought these into our lives, we brought nothing and, and we should remember, we can't take it with us.

I personally believe that we can only receive what we can handle. In other words, stewardship precedes our gifts. A person who does not exercise good stewardship over what he currently has won't be allowed to get additional responsibilities. That is why many times lotto winners end up in the same or worse financial condition than when they started. A person that is a spender will be a spender no matter if he has $100 or $1,000,000. Without changing the mindset, the results stay the same. There are, however, those who are very good stewards over what they currently have and still won't be given more. This symptom is caused by a separate problem. This person's symptom relates to his financial thermostat setting that we discussed in the previous chapter. Although this person learned to be a good steward, he has a thermostat (or attitude) that is set to underachieve. Some have taken care of their apartments with great stewardship; however, they don't have the mindset to handle buying a home. Their thermostats are set to being a tenant as opposed to a landlord.

For instance, if a person is an unsuccessful renter, more than likely without changing their paradigm they will become an unsuccessful homeowner. Many times I ask first-time homebuyers to think about their current apartment to honestly assess whether they were being a good steward over that apartment. A good steward will leave the apartment in the same or better condition than how it was taken.

John Wesley, the father of the doctrinal and practical system of Methodism said, "When the possessor of heaven and earth brought you into being and placed you in this world, he placed you here not as an owner but as a steward—as such he entrusted you for a season with goods of various kinds—but the sole property of these still rests in Him, nor can it ever be alienated from him. As you are not your own, but His, such is likewise all you enjoy."

Stewardship is the science of how people make commonsense decisions regarding money and investing, buying assets and creating wealth. The definition of a steward is a person who manages someone else's property on behalf of the owner. This is done by faithfully applying God's principles to everything with which you have been entrusted.

Remember the three financial blueprints we mentioned in the last chapter? How it's important to find a way to employ a producer's mindset. Matthew 25 reminds us of this very important principle of stewardship. The servant the lord gave five talents to, traded them and made five more. The servant that was given two talents gained two additional talents. But the servant that received one talent went and dug a hole and hid the lord's money. Nevertheless his one talent was taken from him and given to the other servants. Mathew 25:29 says, "for unto every one that hath shall be given, and he shall have abundance; but from him that hath not shall be taken away even that which he hath."

Both of the faithful stewards doubled the money the master had given them and were given the reward. But notice that the money was taken from the third one, who had done the least. Likewise, the better you manage and grow the money with which you have been entrusted, the more money you will have to manage and grow. It's all about stewardship.

Since God is owner, we must realize that we will have possessions only for a short period of time. When we pass away, all our material possessions will remain here on earth. In order to manage many things, we must be found faithful with what we have.

Now consider that *before* we can become a good steward over anything, we must first practice the principle of sowing and reaping. The *fruit* of our success is all about the *root* of our success. Let me ask you this: can a person grow apples by planting orange seeds? We can't expect a harvest without sowing the correct seeds. Sowing seeds of poverty will get you just that, poverty. Sowing seeds of wealth will get you wealth. In order to change the fruit, you must change the root.

# Chapter 4

*Human beings were given a left foot and a right foot to make a mistake*
*first the left, then to the right, left again and repeats.*
Buckminster Fuller
Inventor and Philosopher

### What Happened to the Mortgage Market?

Knowing what happened in the past will prevent you from making some of those same mistakes in the future. The one-word answer to this chapter's title is "**GREED**"! The blame for our current mortgage market can be shared among all parties. I've heard consumers blaming mortgage companies, mortgage companies blaming realtors, the government blaming mortgage brokers, and on and on. The fact of the matter is that all parties had a hand in causing the current mortgage-market situation.

### Wall Street

Wall Street has a single purpose—make money. When investments weren't creating the desired returns, Wall Street investment firms threatened to cease buying mortgage-backed securities. There was pressure to create mortgage products that would encourage more buyers of real estate. Wall Street's appetite for higher-yielding investments increased, and lenders participated with the need of continued purchases from investors.

### Lenders

Lenders caved in to the pressure and created exotic mortgages, minimum-score requirements, and no-money-down programs to encourage home ownership. We had a saying in the industry that went like this, "if a person can fog up a mirror, he can get a mortgage." Usually my seminar audiences get a laugh out of that, but it's a very serious and unfortunate past. Many people who should not have purchased homes were able to have bad credit, no money, and no plan, and still get into a home with zero money down.

### Loan Officers

Unfortunately, some loan officers didn't realize that their clients' interest rates would increase over the first two years of their mortgages. I've had homeowners who have called me for help who started out with a $1,200 payment that increased by $1,000 in two years. To be frank, some loan officers didn't know what they were doing, and others didn't care enough about their clients to make sure their clients were protected. Nearly 65 percent of all loan officers in the years before the meltdown had been in the business for less than three years. I believe in everyone getting a chance, and we all had to start somewhere; however, for this to be the biggest investment in most people's lifetimes, the barrier of entry for loan officers at the time was very low. Many jumped into the mortgage business to simply make money and didn't care to be a student of the business—they were the blind leading the blind. I will spend more time later in this book giving you tips on finding a good mortgage professional.

### Consumers

We are a highly consumptive nation, and we celebrate materialism. Unfortunately, many consumers who bought five-bedroom homes felt they needed to fill every bedroom with furniture and thus used their credit cards to finance it. These five-bedroom homes had two-car garages, and many went out to buy an additional car to fill that too. Many consumers did not work on their credit and thought they could continue life as usual after buying their too-expensive homes. As a homebuyer, you do not have to fill your home with furniture. I remember my good friend, Cheryl Jackson, mentioning that she and her husband waited three or four years before they completed furnishing their home.

It's vitally important that you change your mindset prior to buying your home; your mindset is the key to being a successful homeowner. In addition, because of the housing boom, many homeowners were able to cover up their bad stewardship. They used their home by refinancing to pay off debt once they could not afford to make all of their payments. What do you think happened after that? They went back out and charged up credit cards again with the idea that they would be able to cover it up again by refinancing to pay off debt. This is called debt proliferation and is the downfall of many "consumer-minded" individuals. There is a saying that I like to use to describe this: "When the tide goes out, you find out who is skinny dipping." In other words these homeowners were covering up bad habits by using their homes to continue dipping into their equity to pay off debt. However, the bubble burst or, "the tide went out," and the bad stewards were exposed.

### The Challenge

Our current economic challenge as a whole relates very closely to challenges we are experiencing in our personal economic life. The current economic downturn (national and personal) is largely due to the following.

### Overleverage

Leverage simply means to use OPM to have an advantage. In other words, if I can use another person's or entity's money to help me, then I am leveraged. Banks do it all the time. They borrow your money for .25 percent (if that) and then lend it to a person needing a car loan for 8 percent. Many times, however, borrowing too much money (credit cards for instance) can become a huge problem. Our country has been overleveraged, as have we.

### Lack of Liquidity

Having money saved in an interest-bearing account is advisable. It is suggested that you have six months of your monthly survival number. This survival number is the amount of money you need every month to pay *all* of your bills. Many of the families who have experienced foreclosure may have been all right if they would have had six months of their survival number. This money could have been used as a float account while they tried to sell their home, rent their home or even acquire a roommate. Having six months of your living expenses will help you to be prepared in the event that you fall on hard times.

### Ineffective Regulation System

Our national financial regulation system (the way our government spends and handle money) had been in existence for one hundred years. As you are aware, the current system could no longer sustain itself, thus the mortgage meltdown which led to other problems in our economy. Is your personal economic system broken? Later, you will find a list of ineffective ways to handle your finances. Will you be able to find yourself in any of these?

### Unemployment and the Housing Market

This is the first time in our country's history where home values have declined nationally without a corresponding large rise in unemployment. Many people compared 2007 -2010 to the Great Depression. However, during the Great Depression, the unemployment rate was around 25 percent compared to approximately 10 percent today. Therefore, the challenges being faced today are different than the challenges that were faced in the 1930s.

Today, states like Michigan and Ohio have high rates of unemployment, and this is causing many people in those markets to default on their loans and go into foreclosure. Those markets will not likely rebound until the employment situation improves. On the other hand, home prices in states like Florida, Arizona, and California have declined largely due to unsustainable speculation on the part of investors who overextended themselves by betting that housing prices would always rise.

## Speculative Buying

I personally almost got trapped into making a very bad real estate purchase. I had an opportunity to visit Florida on several occasions while searching for an investment home. I finally found one that I liked and pursued by putting a contract offer on the property. Fortunately the appraisal came in a little lower than the sales price; however, the seller decided to play hardball and didn't want to lower the price. I decided to walk, and it was the best decision that I could have made. The home proceeded to decrease in value and eventually the homes in the area ended up being priced at 50 percent below the price that I was contemplating paying. In other words the home lost 50 percent of its value in a matter of four months. Speculative investing can be a dangerous thing. Markets like Florida have a large glut of investor-owned properties that are going through foreclosure. The downward pressure on housing values due to foreclosures will likely last in most markets across the country for a few years. Larger metropolitan areas such as Washington, DC, are a little more fortunate due to a large government presence. The local unemployment rates for cities like this are lower than the national average. While investing is a good thing, speculative investing may not be the best approach.

*Steady plodding brings prosperity; hasty speculation brings poverty.*
Proverbs 21:5 TLB

*How long will the turmoil in the mortgage markets last?*

The subprime market has virtually evaporated, and lending guidelines have tightened significantly. Interest rates on jumbo mortgages and loans for borrowers with unique situations are considerably higher than loans for borrowers who have smaller mortgage balances, high credit scores, large down payments, and long, steady job histories. There are two factors necessary for lending guidelines to loosen back up: market recovery and clear regulations.

## Housing Market Recovery

Lending guidelines are likely to remain very tight until housing prices at least find a bottom. I do believe we are close to the bottom currently but still have a little way to go. Lenders and mortgage insurance companies and Wall Street investors don't want to assume the risk that homeowners will walk away from their mortgage if the home declines in value.

## Clear Rules and Regulations

Lenders and Wall Street investors today are very hesitant to be flexible in their guidelines as long as the rules of the games are still undefined. There is a very large fear in the marketplace among banks and mortgage lenders that they will be faced with large legal liability if they extend loans to people who may not be able to afford the payments at some point in the future.

*Is this a good time to buy a home?*

Absolutely! This is definitely a buyer's market! Your negotiating power in this market is greater than at any point in the last several years. If you are interested in buying a home for the long term, I believe this may be the opportunity of a lifetime. Many times when interest rates are low, home prices are high and vice versa. In the market today, we have experienced record low rates and bottom level home prices.

Many buyers express interest in real estate investing. Although I believe Real Estate is one of the best ways to increase your passive income and build wealth, being very careful in the word of real estate investing is a must, especially in this market. If you are a novice looking to speculate in the real estate markets, now may be the worst time to do so because this current market is more dangerous than ever. Only the truly savvy investors will be able to navigate the market today, but they need to act quickly. There is so much panic selling in the marketplace right now that the deals that are available today will not likely be around in the future. Of course, there will always be deals available, but the types of deals available today are not going to last forever. Warren Buffet has often said to buy low and sell high. Everyone talks about buying low and selling high, but hardly anyone actually does it. Once the market stabilizes, everyone will want to jump in again, and the best deals will have disappeared.

The best thing for you to do is work with a team of professionals to help you structure your home-purchase transaction in ways where you could save the most money. Strategies for you to consider include seller-paid closing costs, maximizing your leverage (using other people's money OPM), created tax benefits, structuring the down payment in the proper way, strategic financing, viable down payment assistance programs, and other useful strategies.

Before purchasing a home, you may want to make sure your personal system is analyzed for effectiveness. If you notice, some of the same problems our nation has suffered through closely relates to one's personal system. It may be a good idea to determine if your personal system is outdated and ineffective. The following is a list of examples of a system that may be flawed.

### Examples of an Ineffective Personal System

### Using an ATM Card Frequently

This is a definite no-no. For one, if you are using your ATM frequently, there is a high probability that you are not balancing your checkbook. Also, you may be racking up fees for using your own money.

### Not Completing a Monthly Budget

How do you know where you are going without a road map? A budget is your road map to financial success. Unless the family has an organized and detailed plan for spending, they will more than likely have problems with overspending. I challenge you to start a budge this week!

### Shopping for a Mortgage Incorrectly

The question most often asked by homebuyers is "what is your interest rate?" Although that is a good question, you'll learn to ask better questions in Chapter 18.

### Paying Credit Cards after the Due Date

$25 to $50 late fee…Enough said!

### Not Balancing the Checkbook

If you are not balancing your checkbook, how do you know how much you have? This is a fundamental activity to being a successful financial steward. You should *always* know how much money you have.

### Paying the Mortgage after the Sixteenth of the Month

Question: When is your payment due? If you answered "by the sixteenth," then you are wrong! Your payment is due on the first of each month. The lender gives you a grace period until the fifteenth of the month, after which it will cost you 4 percent of your payment.

### Cashing Your Paycheck Immediately

One way to spend your money quickly is to have it available. Conversely, if it's not available in your account, well guess what? You can't spend it! This of course would not work if you have direct deposit.

### Not Spending Time Reviewing Assets

One hour a month is recommended to review all assets. One person should be the CFO, if married, and should be responsible for calling a monthly financial meeting. Earlier, if you recall, I compared owning a home to owning a business.

## Using your Home as your Local ATM (Automated Teller-Machine)

For current homeowners, using equity in the property has been a downfall. Your equity is not to be consumed; it should only be used to conserve and to grow your asset base.

Conversely, there may be some effective ways that will help you meet your financial and mortgage goals.

## Examples of an Effective Personal System

## Implement the Two-Week Rule before Purchase

I guarantee if you implement this rule it will save you quite a bit over the next year. Why don't you implement a cooling-off period of two weeks before you buy anything? If the urge to buy that item has not dissipated, then go back and buy it. I am hoping, however that the need to buy will dissipate. Many people are compulsive shoppers. If you put yourself on a "system" you may be able to save a little money.

## 10 Percent Tithe or Contribution

If you are tithing, please continue. I think this is the most important aspect of your financial life. Do not let buying a home get in the way of your instruction. Malachi 3:10 says, "Bring the full tithes into the storehouse, that there may be food in my house; and thereby put me to the test, says the Lord of hosts, if I will not open the windows of heaven for you and pour down for you an overflowing blessing."

If you are not tithing, I would strongly suggest that you consider it. Many of the world's wealthiest individuals and most successful people have been devout tithers. Even Fortune 500 companies understand the principle of sowing and reaping. They give millions of dollars away annually to causes that they believe in and reap benefits in return. We see this principle at work in the world. Think about the philanthropist who creates a foundation, even though the motivation may be to save on taxes, The principle still works. Consider even the businessman who puts money into a new business venture with the expectation of receiving a return. The law of sowing and reaping will work for every person who uses it.

### Save 10 Percent of Gross

I will admit, saving 10 percent of your gross can be easier said than done; however, try to max out your 401(k) if your employer is matching. You are tasked with living off of 80 percent of your income. With a tight budget and preparation, I believe you can do it. It may take a sacrifice, but it's time to do whatever it takes. You future financial life is more important than the latest gadget, expensive purse, or new shoes. Most people won't be able to retire at the appropriate age. Will that be you? I hope not! Go ahead and make the changes today so that you can live a comfortable life during your latter years. You can do it!

### Identify One Spouse as the CFO

Your home is your business. In any business you have a CEO and a CFO. Appoint one person, if you are married, to be the Chief Financial Officer. That person should be in charge of bringing the information together for a monthly meeting with the other partner. The business (your home) cannot travel in two different directions. Your home should run like a well-oiled machine. There should be a financial meeting for a minimum of one hour per month with the partners to discuss income, expenditures, and assets.

### Have a Relationship with Financial Professionals

In the multitude of counselors there is safety. When you align yourself with strong financial minds, you make yourself available for new information. I would advise that you always have your team of professionals saved on your phone, including your mortgage professional, financial advisor, tax consultant, insurance agent, estate planner, lawyer, and realtor. That is the only way you'll have access to information when you need it. The most successful people surround themselves with professionals who are qualified and effective. Start getting your professional team in order today. In addition, at some point you may want to call a meeting for all of your professionals to meet together. There's nothing like having your own professional team (who all have your best interests at heart) working in unison on your behalf.

### Have Written 5 Year Financial Plan

A written plan is crucial to be able to see where you are going. This plan does not have to be elaborate. It can be as simple as determining how much money you want in your savings in five years, what major purchases you may need to make, etc. You may have a five-year debt elimination plan. Again, this plan doesn't necessarily have to be complete. As you pursue your goals, the road you are traveling may curve. However, you at least should have a tentative plan on how you will hit your mark. You may even want to start with a shorter time frame, say three years.

### Know Your Monthly Survival Number

Your survival number is the income needed to make all of your bill payments per month. The goal is to save three to six months of this survival number. Not only should you know the amount of money needed to meet your living needs every month(called your survival number), but at some point you should save your survival number in an interest-bearing account. This account is not a vacation or "splurge" account. It has a specific purpose that is for emergencies only. If you have this survival number already saved, you may be able to smooth out the rough periods. Just think how much better some of the homeowners going through foreclosure would have been if they simply followed this one instruction. Save six months of your living expenses.

## Work on Your Credit and Credit Score

I suggest you request a copy of your credit report every six months. Always look to try to increase or improve your score (discussed in a later chapter). Keep credit balances at 30 percent or below the allowed credit limit. Stay out of the department stores and guard your credit like a watchdog.

## Give Yourself a Specific Monthly Allowance

Too many people spend the money they have available. Set yourself on a specific monthly budget. Once you meet your allowance amount, guess what? You are done for the month.

## Use a Credit Card for Purchases over $20 and Pay Off Monthly

Larger purchases can be put on a credit card to be paid off *completely* at the end of the month.

## How to Successfully Get a Mortgage in 2012 and Beyond

Getting a mortgage in 2011 and beyond will be a little more complicated than it has been in the past because of the challenging economy and increased government regulation of the mortgage industry. As a matter of fact, it is as challenging as I've experienced over my seventeen-year career. Currently it's like a giant hurricane has swept through the housing, financial, and mortgage markets, leaving chunks of debris in its wake. But never fear (remember the four enemies of life I wrote about earlier), that's why you have certified professionals to navigate you through this exciting experience. Here are a few of the challenges that we will tackle together as we navigate the danger zone known as the mortgage process!

## New Good Faith Estimate

The US government has created a new version of the disclosure form known as the Good Faith Estimate (GFE). The old GFE itemized all your closing costs and illustrated your "cash-to-close"—the amount of cash you would need to bring to the closing if you are buying a home or the net proceeds you would receive at the closing from a cash-out refinance. The new GFE lumps in your closing costs under certain categories instead of itemizing them and does not illustrate your cash-to close. Also, if the seller is paying closing costs or points on your behalf, this is not reflected on the new GFE. In other words, it will look as though you are paying these fees even though the seller is paying them.

### New Appraisal Guidelines

Most mortgage loans in this current market are either insured by the Federal Housing Administration (FHA) or sold to Fannie Mae or Freddie Mac. This means that mortgage banks and brokers need to follow the rules set by Fannie, Freddie, and the FHA. In 2009, Fannie and Freddie adopted new rules surrounding the home appraisal process. In 2010, the FHA followed suit and implemented many of the same guidelines. What this means for you as the home buyer is that the appraisal process is going to be more stringent and inflexible, costly, and time consuming than it has been in the past.

Many appraisals are now conducted by appraisers who may not live in your community, resulting in value estimates that may not agree with your own opinion of what the home you want to buy may be worth. Also, many appraisals now go through multiple layers of screening and are handled by an appraisal management company. In addition, loan originators are prohibited in most cases from ordering appraisals or communicating directly with appraisers. Even so, it is important to keep in mind that an appraisal is simply an opinion of what the home you want to buy would sell for in today's market. You and I are entitled to disagree with the appraiser, but the lending guidelines that we need to follow require us to use the appraiser's opinion when calculating your loan amount and strategy.

**New Disclosure Rules**

The US Congress has enacted some new laws, and the Federal Reserve Board has issued some new guidelines that could delay the loan process. For instance, if the APR (Annual Percentage Rate) on your loan changes by more than .125 percent before the closing, the lender needs to issue new disclosure forms and give you time to review the new forms.

**Here are a few examples of things that could cause the APR to change:**

- You decide to lock in your interest rate or get a rate lock extension
- You decide to reduce your loan amount
- You are getting an adjustable rate mortgage and the index value changes
- Your credit score changes before closing, resulting in a higher rate or higher fees
- You decide to pay more or less points than what you initially requested
- 

**Higher Credit Score Guidelines**

Prior to the Mortgage Crisis, clients with little money and low credit scores (as low as 580) were still able to get a mortgage loan. I know it sounds ridiculous, but if your current credit score is less than 700, you may get hit with higher fees if your loan is being sold to Fannie or Freddie. If your score is 620 or better, you are still able to get an FHA loan. Yet, recently I've seen investors raise their minimum credit score standards to 640. One thing that has caused many consumer scores to decrease is that some credit card companies have reduced the credit limits on accounts that have never even been late. This is causing credit scores to go down across the board for people who have never been late on any payments in their life! If you fall into this category, or if you have some challenges with your credit score, you may get hit with higher costs when it comes to getting a mortgage.

# Chapter 5

---

*Life is like a combination lock; your job is to find the right numbers, in the right order, so you can have anything you want.*
Brian Tracy
Author and Motivational speaker

### Assessing Your Profile

Once you have decided to take action, you'll need to start getting feedback about your current financial situation. You'll get data, advice, help, suggestions, direction, and even constructive criticism that will help you constantly adjust and move forward while continually enhancing your borrowing profile. Sometimes we tend not to like negative feedback; however, there is as much useful data in negative feedback as there is in positive feedback. It tells us that we are off course, headed in the wrong direction, or doing the wrong thing.

If it is determined that you will need to make some adjustments to improve your buying potential, beginning in small, manageable steps gives you a greater chance of long-term success. Doing too much too fast not only overwhelms you, it also can reverse your effort and possibly cause failure, thereby reinforcing the belief that it's too difficult, if not impossible. When you start with small, achievable steps, it reinforces your commitment and belief that you can make the necessary changes.

### How Your Profile Is Rated

Having a mind to build is the initial stage of home stewardship. Once we have established a solid foundation for the project, it is now time to survey the land. Making an accurate assessment of your current buying power prior to application is essential.

The mortgage company will make an assessment of your financial status before going forward. There are many ways to enter into a mortgage, but finding the avenue that is best for you is my top priority. This information is most helpful for you as a buyer because it gives you a general idea of what mortgage professionals look for to qualify you for the right loan. The evaluation of your profile will give you an idea of what areas you are strong in and the areas where your weaknesses can be strengthened.

With that in mind, let us begin to look at the two types of profiles a homebuyer may have: "has money" or "no money." To give you an even better idea of what will be analyzed when qualifying a prospective buyer, we're going to look at these two by breaking each profile down into three categories:

- Category I—Perfect Credit
- Category II—Challenging Credit
- Category III—No Credit

## Category I

**Perfect Credit *with No* Money for Down Payment and Closing Costs**

**High Debt**

If a buyer has perfect credit, this means that his/her credit score is generally rated between 680 and 700. The borrower's capacity to support repayment of the mortgage is evident based on her past payment history. This means that we are most likely to rate this person as a leading candidate for immediate home stewardship with little to no problems when it comes to getting the loan approved.

This profile tells the lender that the borrower understands that credit is the most important aspect of securing a loan. However, the high-debt status speaks to the fact that she is also most likely to start spending and using open lines of credit. If this is you, it is critical for you to stop using credit cards immediately. As a suggestion, I recommend that you terminate all credit cards with the exception of only one that will be used in case of an emergency. It may also be good for you to contact your local bank or credit union and work toward consolidating your debt. You are still in good shape as a potential buyer because you have a proven track record of maintaining a good and solid credit repayment history.

During this time, you should not add to the already high amount of debt you have accumulated. Also, I would highly recommend that you start a small savings account as well.

**Low Debt**

Perfect credit speaks to your ability to honor a credit agreement and shows a proven history of repaying a loan. More important, it shows the character, integrity, and manner in which you are able to prioritize your expenditures. This is extremely favorable when the lender looks at how much of a risk they would be taking when approving a loan for your new home. See budget sheet in workbook

A perfect credit–low debt profile reflects a person who handles debt obligations extremely well. It tells the lender that you understand the value of keeping debts low, and you have learned to properly manage credit through either listening to advice or through trial and error. However, the fact that you may not have any available cash (savings) may tell us that you have been unable to save properly and may need to analyze spending habits. I would recommend a thirty-day budget to obtain an accurate picture if this is a true statement.

In this example, you will need little or no money down when buying your home. Coming up with financial investment for earnest-money deposit (the deposit made in order to submit your offer, usually

1% of the purchase price) may be difficult if you haven't been able to save. If this scenario describes you, you may want to get on a savings fast track. In addition, be prepared to pay for the upfront cost of buying ( i.e credit report, appraisal, Home Inspections, Homeowners Insurance).

I suggests that you revisit your methods of saving and come up with a reasonable and concrete way to store money before buying. I don't want you to get into the house and end up losing it down the line because of unforeseen emergencies. I highly recommend that you find a way to put away the equivalent of at least three mortgage payments in case of an emergency before buying a home.

### Perfect Credit *with* Money for Down Payment and Closing Costs

### High Debt

We have looked at the profile of a potential homebuyer with little or no money to work with. Now we're going to look at a perfect credit–high debt profile with money. This category is generally reserved for people who understand their credit responsibility but have gone a little overboard in spending. This category also indicates that you may be a shopper, and that most likely, you enjoy the finer things in life. That usually explains having high debt or open lines of credit. One of the things you may have a problem with is putting an end to your shopping habit.

Shopping isn't limited to clothing. This profile speaks of a person who enjoys eating out at five-star restaurants regularly, interior decorating, constant home improvement, detailing vehicles, and other high-quality lifestyle choices that usually lead to high debt. People who fall in this category are often unaware of how many credit cards they have.

I suggest that you use your money to pay off existing debt and eliminate all credit cards with the exception of one for emergencies. I know this may seem unthinkable and even unreasonable, but you can do it. You may be reluctant to stop using your credit cards, but always remember: persistence overcomes resistance. You can and will overcome the high-debt profile. I recommend a nine-month "stop spending" fast. Yes, a debt diet or fast. It has proven to work with not only eliminating unnecessary debt but also giving you the chance to take control of your life through modified spending while developing discipline and sound decision making.

### Low Debt

If low debt accurately describes your credit profile, you are in the absolute-best scenario possible for a potential homebuyer. One or two things have taken place: you have learned from trial and error or you have employed wisdom and sound advice. Either way, you have become a very-low-risk applicant.

You probably pay off all credit card balances by the end of each month. You also review your credit report at least once a year for accuracy. As a result, you have the option of putting money down or going into a loan by bringing absolutely nothing to the table. Additionally, you are most likely to have the finances to cover the closing costs without the assistance of the seller. Clearly, you are on your way to becoming a very successful home steward.

### Category II

### Challenging Credit *with No* Money for Down Payment and Closing Costs

### High Debt

A person with challenging credit is defined as one who has experienced one or a series of unfortunate circumstances that may be categorized as life-changing events. In most cases you have experienced dramatic financial setbacks due to divorce, decrease in salary, unemployment, or personal or family illness. Having challenging credit could also indicate your inability to repay a loan properly, failure to communicate with creditors, or unsound financial decision making when it comes to appropriating funds.

Whatever the reason that has led you to have challenging credit, I strongly believe that your name can be restored and you can reestablish yourself as a creditable candidate for a mortgage loan. There is no reason to be discouraged, as life happens to us all, and we have all made bad decisions at some point in our lives. There is a way out of your circumstance.

One of the most important things you have to understand about credit is that our names, our reputations, are all we have. When a company is looking to extend a loan to a potential client, they don't make the decision based on a personal relationship or through personal references. Instead, they look to your credit profile, which tells them everything they need to know about your character and priorities. It gives them a very good idea of the risk involved in extending credit to you. How you have repaid prior loans or honored prior commitments will speak directly to how you intend to pay them back. Our word isn't good enough anymore; the proof is in the pudding, so to speak.

Here are some helpful tools that I recommend you employ in order to redeem yourself. Redemption deals with buying back. You must be of the mindset that you have to buy back what you already own. Your name was great at one time, and now is your chance to buy it back. That's the only way your credit—and your name—can be restored.

Contact your creditors immediately and let them know your situation. Request them to send you an itemized statement of all charges or validation of the debt. Let them know that you are taking steps to restore your credit and that you will need this information to get started. If your account is now with a third-party collection agency, be sure to contact the collector or the attorney's office handling the case and have them request this information from the client. Also let them know your intention. They will usually place a thirty-day hold on the account while they investigate and forward the information to you.

Write all of your bills down along with payments, interest rates, and balances. Keep in mind that you owe the balance in full. Although you may have spent only $500 in purchases, the addition of late fees, interest, and collection costs have resulted in a higher balance. Disputing the interest is a losing battle. Once you activated and used the card, you agreed to the terms of the agreement. Whether you signed an agreement or used the credit card, you are legally obligated to honor the terms of the agreement.

I would suggest that you obtain budget and credit counseling to gain a better understanding of your credit and to get other helpful tools on how you can restore it while eliminating your high-debt profile.

**Low Debt**

If you fall into the low-debt category, it is likely that you don't have current bills outside of immediate payments like gas and electric. Most of your bills may be connected to charge-off accounts. It is likely that you use a cash-and-carrying system and may find it difficult to keep your debt current, and you may have credit challenges because of your past accounts. I would suggest that you obtain a copy of your credit report with the mindset that you must pay debts! I highly recommend that you lean heavily toward developing strict discipline toward savings, and you may want to consider free credit counseling to make sure your mindset has changed toward credit and debt.

The fact that an account has been charged off doesn't release you from your obligation to honor the agreement. By law, the creditor is required to report your payments or non-payments. Once you have failed to repay the loan within 120 days, your account will be charged off and may be sent to a collection agency or collection law firm for further action. Contrary to popular belief, you can be sued for the balance in full, the interest, and attorney fees. Once a judgment is secured against you, it will stay on your credit for seven to ten years and may count forty points or more against your credit score. A judgment is public record, which means that if a security clearance is required for a job, it will appear. Additionally, a judgment may be executed within thirty days. If a judgment is executed against you, your bank account may be immediately frozen, a lien may be placed against your personal property, and your wages may be garnished. In some states, your income taxes may be withheld until the balance is paid in full.

More and more creditors are hiring collection law firms to secure repayment of credit card and commercial debt. You must act now if you are going to restore your credit. The only way to have the interest waived is to agree to settle the account with a lump-sum payment that usually exceeds 60 percent of the balance. The attorney or collection agency is not obligated to give you a discount off the debt. It is the discretion of the firm or agency to qualify you and approve a settlement to release you from the debt. Any time you enter into an agreement with a creditor or attorney's office, be sure to get a receipt and a confirmation of any verbal agreement. Once the debt is paid, request a $0.00 balance statement. Also, before sending any form of payment for a settlement, request a release-of-obligation letter from the creditor, agency, or law firm. Debts are often sold to other agencies, and you may be called again to pay the remaining balance because sometimes settlements are not reported accurately. You will need this information when disputing any "paid prior" disputes with credit reporting agencies.

You may want to prioritize your debts by the highest interest rates. Pay as much as you can into the principle balance, and the creditor may agree to reduce the interest after you show good faith in resolving the debt. This may not be true for accounts with law firms because their focus is on collecting the balance in full or the most possible at one time. Nevertheless, make this your focal point. Keep a close watch on your finances every week. You will have to micromanage every account down to the cent. You may also want to contact the nearest nonprofit counseling agency to get help and information on paying your bills.

I would not necessarily recommend debt-settlement companies. They have limited power of attorney and can only negotiate settlements. They will charge you a fee for their services. You will send payments to them monthly, and they will promise to hold them in a savings account until you have accumulated enough to offer each creditor a settlement. The first few payments will go to their fee. This is not a good idea for accounts that have not been charged off. Keep in mind that your creditors have mandatory reporting requirements. Their agreement is with you and not with a debt-settlement company. Regardless of what the debt-settlement company tells you, the creditor cannot legally agree to the terms and conditions of their system because the money that you send to the debt-settlement company is being reported by your creditor as nonpayment. After a few months, your account will be charged off.

Debt-settlement companies work best for situations where all of your accounts are charged off. However, your inability to save money is what will cost you in the end. You may have to pay a debt-settlement company $1500 in fees just to save the money and negotiate a settlement on your behalf. Ultimately this is a decision you have to make. I want you to be as knowledgeable as possible when restoring your credit. In the event that you decide to hire the services of a debt-settlement company, you will not only prolong your ability to restore your credit and buy a home, you will also run the risk of still being sued by a law firm, who may secure an arbitration award against you and ultimately obtain a judgment. Many creditors are requiring mandatory arbitration instead of litigation in their agreements. This is why you want to request a copy of the original application so that you can review the fine print when looking to restore your credit.

## Challenging Credit *with* Money for Down Payment and Closing Costs

### High Debt

The difference between one with challenging credit–high debt and one who has perfect credit is very simple. The person with perfect credit uses her money to pay her bills. On the other hand, if you are in this category you may hold on to the money instead of paying the bills consistently. Considering the fact that you have a healthy cash flow, there has been no reason to categorize yourself as one with credit challenges until now. As you prepare to petition a lender to grant you a home loan, for the first time your credit has presented a challenge for you.

You more than likely live pretty well and are financially comfortable, although in the past you may have experienced difficulty and worked to overcome any problems with your finances. While you have money, you haven't adequately appropriated it to meet your financial obligations for whatever reason. As a result, you may have had trouble receiving new credit recently. If you are able to get hold of this minor problem, you are well on your way to becoming a successful new home steward.

Based on your profile, you will not have a problem coming up with a down payment, covering closing costs and the appraisal, and paying for the credit report. Again, you are well on your way to becoming a very successful new home steward if you can get a handle on your payment history immediately. Making a very small change can result in possibly improving the interest rate you will receive when you're ready to purchase. Interest rates can make a very big difference in your monthly payment.

I suggest that you make sure to invest in your company's 401(k) program, catch up on your delinquent accounts, and begin paying them on time immediately. If you are able to implement these changes, your debt-ratio lines will become more favorable to the bank. You may also want to consider a consolidation loan to combine your credit card balances with cards that have lower rates. Also be sure to decline any future credit card offers extended to you as it may negatively affect your profile during this very important evaluation of your credit report by the lender.

### Low Debt

If you fall into this low-debt category, bankruptcy, judgments, collections, current past-due accounts, and previous past-due accounts have negatively impacted your credit profile.

Although you've experienced slipups in the past, you understand the importance of not having too many debt accounts. You have managed to stay away from a lot of credit but will need to work to clear up credit challenges from the past. A person that fits this profile generally has recent payment problems, current past-due accounts, and a low credit score. While you have been able to sustain a stable job, you will need to find a way to begin paying off the delinquent debt.

You should not have a problem coming up with the money needed for a down payment and closing costs, but based on your profile, I believe it will be in your best interest to use that money to pay off any collections or judgments. Some of the collections (under $1,000) can be left open without payment in some instances; however, all accounts over this amount will have to be paid off in order to move forward with the loan application.

### Category III

### No Credit

If you are in the no-credit category, open at least one credit card for emergency purposes. In order to receive credit for your account, you will need to use your card at least once a month and pay it off in full each month. You may want to try going to a local bank or credit union and leverage your savings account with getting a secured credit card. Make sure to obtain a copy of all cancelled checks over the last twelve months for rental payments. Also be sure to have your nontraditional creditors (car insurance, mobile phone, utilities etc) provide payment history verification letters. All in all, you want to keep track of all receipts for payments made to creditors for your own record. These things can be very effective when trying to establish a verifiable credit history for a lender.

If you are of the mindset of carrying cash as a method of buying, you are likely to have little to no credit established. While paying cash is clearly the best way to go, it may also hinder you from obtaining credit. Unless you are in a position to pay cash for a car, house, or other things that most of us have to finance, you will need to develop a credit history by financing a personal loan, opening a secured credit card, or saving enough money to use as a down payment on a vehicle. The repayment of credit will be recorded and will give lenders the profile they need when determining your risk factor.

It is important that you keep paying your rent on time. Continue to pay every creditor on time. Start a savings account and establish good credit. Correct credit issues and try to settle as many accounts as possible. In the event that you are able to come up with a lump sum of money, contact your creditors and offer 50–60 percent settlements. Before doing this, make sure you obtain the total amount due so that you can make the best possible offer. You will also want to request that they remove negative items from your report once the balance is satisfied. Begin putting your money into an above-average interest bearing account.

# Chapter 6

*The will to win is nothing without the will to prepare.*
Author Unknown

## Preparing for the Loan Interview

While preparing for the interview process, you must first determine which mortgage program works best for you and also be aware of the various costs involved when buying. You will read in chapter 12, "Counting the Cost of Home Stewardship," which will give you more detailed information on the costs involved. Prior to meeting with a mortgage loan officer, you'll need to know what to expect. There are upfront costs, down-payment cost, and closing costs that you will need to be prepared for.

Review your reasons for buying (see workbook) and determine whether you are ready to do what is needed to become a home steward. The more valid reasons you can come up with to buy a home, the better your chances of having success. Without purpose as the compass to guide you, your goals and home-buying desires may not ultimately satisfy you. You don't want to get to the top of the ladder only to find out you had it leaning up against the wrong wall. For my first-time homebuyers, I sometimes start with an exercise geared toward getting down to the foundational reasons for this large purchase. Usually I find that the very first reason someone gives me is superficial. In order to get a deeper connection with the buying decision, I continue to ask "why" questions. I usually take notes on each client so that I can truly understand what's important to them. Here is the dialogue from one of my clients, Ms. James:

- **Me**: Why is buying this home important to you, Ms. James?
- **Ms. James**: Because I want a larger space for my family.
- **Me**: Why is it important to have a larger space for your family?
- **Ms. James**: Most of my family were renters and we had very little space.
- **Me**: Why is it important to live in a home as oppose to a bigger apartment?
- **Ms. James**: I don't want my children to rent.
- **Me**: So it's important for your children to understand the importance of ownership?
- **Ms James**: Yes, and they can start with this home.
- **Me**: Why is it important for them to begin with this home?
- **Ms James**: I want to leave something here for my children and hope that they will do the same for their children.

Did you notice the transformation? Ms. James didn't simply want to buy a home for more space. That was a reason, but there was more to it. Her real reason for this sacrificial decision was about leaving an inheritance for her children. As a matter of fact, she wanted this to be a start of the blessing to her children's children!

Now that you are connected with your purpose of buying this home, let's talk about getting qualified. Once you've been prequalified by phone, this is the time to start thinking about needs, wants, and areas of interest. Keep in mind, buying a home is relative. For example, moving into a high-tax area will result in your payments being high. One of my five keys to having a successful home-buying experience is to "be realistic." If your goal, for instance, is to pay $600 per month, you will get a home worth $600 per month. You should take into consideration your budget, the minimum down payment, your maximum monthly mortgage payment, and closing costs when choosing your home. Also a good rule of thumb that has been used over the years to determine your price range is 2.5 to 3.0 times your salary (e.g., if your yearly total income is $60,000, then your target purchase price would be approximately $180,000).

You must also review your financial situation. Understand that there are three costs when buying a home: upfront cost, the down payment and closing costs. Prior to the loan interview, you'll need to determine how much you set aside for these costs. Keep in mind your closing costs will depend on the program that works best for you, interest rates at the time, and the existing market. I suggest that you take some time to determine the maximum amount of money you have to invest into your home. How about your monthly payment comfort zone? You'll need to determine how much you can realistically afford for your monthly payment. This is called the periodic cost of buying a home and should be determined up front.

As you may know, buying a home is a long-term investment. Home stewardship requires a great deal of commitment from you, so I suggest writing down your goals for buying—from where you would like to live to how much you would like to pay. Writing down your goals is important because it tattoos your desires on your brain, so to speak. When you write your goals you essentially create your future in advance. During this preparation stage, you will need to get as much leverage as you can on yourself. Many people give up during this process simply because they had not anchored their goal with the right reasons for taking this journey. Do you think that Ms. James, in the above scenario lost her zeal to find her home? Absolutely not; she pressed until she met her goal. Her reason for buying a home was tied to her children and their future. Talking about leverage, she wanted to leave a deposit here on earth for her children, and it went beyond the physical home. She wanted her children to understand the importance of investing in an asset and not be tied to the bondage of renting.

Making an accurate financial analysis of all income and distribution of funds over the past twelve months would be an effective preparation task. Determine if there are several different sources of income that you depend upon. Have there been changes in your income over the past year? Do you expect changes in your in your income for the coming year? Keep in mind, the way you appropriated funds over the last twelve months gives a very good assessment of how you may handle your finances over the next twelve months. This is critical when it comes to investing in the purchase of a new home. This will be a perfect time to modify your behavior for the best. ***Many people want to change without changing.***

I suggest that you review your budget (or create a budget) and make any and all adjustments necessary to curb spending and get prepared for the financial investment that will be required as you pursue home stewardship. I often suggest that first-time homebuyers make a concerted effort to keep meticulous records of all spending for a period of time (e.g., ninety days) to get a firm grip on your spending habits and money paradigm. I believe this process will identify areas that you will need to change to be prepared for the monthly mortgage payment.

In the event that you have not been able to manage your money properly, now is the ideal time to get started on a healthy diet of money management. If you've been having problems in this area, then it is vitally important that you change your mindset about handling money *before* you buy your home. Your financial success can only grow to the extent that you do! I suggest that your objective should be to overcome the obstacles that get in your way of creating financial success. Ask yourself this: "If I were the mortgage company, would I lend myself the money needed to buy a home?" I wish I could be in your thoughts right now. Usually when I ask that question to buyers, I simply get a smile. If the answer is no, your job is simple. One of the biggest differences between financial success and financial failure is how well you manage your income and money. To master your money, you must manage your money**!**

Be sure that you make an educated and practical decision when deciding on a home. Remember that you can change everything about a home except its location. Be sure to conduct an extensive study of the area before agreeing on a contract. Buying a home is not like shopping for a pair of shoes. You don't have to wear those shoes if they don't look as good as they did in the store window. However, home stewardship is different. You not only have to live *in* the decision you made but you will also have to continue to make payments for a long time *on* that decision that you made. My Episcopal Pastor's wife, Reverend Diana P. Cherry, coined a phrase many years ago, "choices are long lasting and life changing." In other words we are required to live with our decisions, good, bad, or indifferent. Be sure to make the best possible decision when preparing for this commitment.

It is also good to have an idea of how long you plan to live in the home. The length of time you expect to live in the home will directly affect the financing options, size of the home, and the location. A few things you may want to consider when making an assessment of how long you want to live in a property include marriage, children, job location, aging parent you may have to care for, schools, cycle of life, and type of community. According to the National Association of Realtors, five to seven years is the average time of occupation for first-time homebuyers, which is another reason why thinking that your first home is "the only house for me" may not be a plausible approach to buying.

When preparing for the interview, there are certain documents that you will need to take to your appointment. As I mentioned earlier, one of the enemies in life is disorganization. Preparing for the interview will help you to get more organized. It will be advisable to gather your documents in advance and not wait until the last minute to get the required items together. If you can make copies of your documents or simply print electronic versions, that will help the process move smoothly.

### Items you will need at application

- Pay stubs for the last month
- The last two years W-2 forms
- The last two years 1040 tax returns including all schedules
- The last two months bank statements

- The last two months (or last quarter) asset accounts (Thrifts, 401(k), 403(b), mutual funds, nonqualified retirement accounts, etc.)
- Copy of your driver's license and social security card
- Name and number of your current landlord for verification (if you have the last twelve months cancelled checks, that would be even better)
- Name and number of contact from your human resources department
- 

Having all of these documents ready for application will help speed up the process. If you have any questions about these documents, you should contact your mortgage loan officer immediately to get clarity.

## The Home-Loan Process

### 1)    Seek God

Matthew 6:33 says, "seek ye first the kingdom of God and His righteousness and all these things will be added unto you." I firmly believe that prayer sets the foundation and direction for every decision. I also believe that it's important to have a clear direction before you start your quest toward home stewardship

### 2)    Get Counsel

When I purchased my home, there weren't organizations to help me with the understanding of the process. I simply meandered through the process and somehow ended up at the closing signing papers with fear and trembling. You, however, are very fortunate to have nonprofit agencies who care about your well-being. These agencies specialize in educating you through one-on-one counseling, group training, etc. My counsel would be to get counsel. In the multitude of counselors, there is safety.

### 3)    Prequalification

Prequalification involves a verbal conversation over the phone, usually with a mortgage loan officer. A standard application would be completed to ascertain basic information to determine eligibility and affordability. Be prepared to share income, asset, and employment information with the mortgage loan officer. In addition, a credit report will need to be requested and reviewed. Sometimes the mortgage loan officer may only pull a one-bureau credit report to get a snapshot of your qualification. However, it's best to make sure he has pulled a tri-merged credit report to understand the entire picture. Sometimes pulling one credit report will give a score that may not necessarily be a representative of the middle score, which is the score that the underwriter will use to determine your qualification.

### 4)    Preapproval

Preapproval is a more formal commitment to lend. It takes into consideration written evidence of what was shared with the mortgage loan officer by phone. Usually your information will be run through an underwriting portal called Desktop Underwriter to get a written preapproval on your loan request. A preapproval is a little stronger than a prequalification. Many times an underwriter will not underwrite a file without having an address. However, with the advent of Desktop Underwriter, your file can be analyzed by a sophisticated underwriting portal that will determine your eligibility without having a specific property.

### 5)    Formal Loan Application

You will eventually sit down face to face with a mortgage loan officer, or at least I hope you will. It's important to be able to meet the person on the other side of the phone. In the old days, every transaction was done face to face. This may be the biggest investment in your lifetime. Why not be certain to sit down with your mortgage loan officer to sign pertinent documents to get your loan processing started? Your application meeting will last for approximately one hour. Updated documents will be collected and you'll sign disclosure documents to get your loan processed.

## 6)    Processing

Your loan file will be updated if necessary and verified through various checks and balances. The processor's job essentially is to minimize any weakness of your profile and to accentuate all strengths you may have. Your entire profile will be verified, confirmed, and packaged for underwriting. The processor will look to verify two years of employment, two years of work history, the last two months of average balance in your bank account, social security number, credit report, tax returns, W-2 forms, income, deductions, etc.

## 7)    Underwriting

This is the decision-making step. A qualified underwriter will review your file and essentially verify everything that the processor has done on your file. His job is simply to confirm that your profile meets the standards of the particular loan type that you are applying for.

## 8)    Celebration

Some people call this settlement. I like to call this the celebration. You will attend a closing at the settlement company's office, the realtor's office, or the mortgage loan officer's office. All parties attend the closing. There will be stacks of documents for you to review and sign. Sometimes the celebration settlement is short and sometimes it takes a long time. You will need a certified check for monies needed, a copy of your driver's license, and any other documents your mortgage loan officer has requested.

Even more important than completing the transaction, the simple, enjoyable act of acknowledging and rewarding your success causes your subconscious mind to connect hard work, commitment, and sacrifice to the reward. Celebrating your success gives you a sense of accomplishment and recognition. After closing, treat yourself out because you deserve it!

The commitment to repaying a mortgage loan is a very serious one. It is important to remember that there is no such thing as "this is the only house for me." It may be wise to purchase a less expensive home or what we consider a "starter home" in your initial buying experience. The best time to buy a home depends on one variable. You!

# Chapter 7

*Every great leap forward in your life comes after you made a clear decision of some kind.*
Brian Tracy

### Prequalifying for Your Loan

After you've adopted the correct mindset and analyzed your current financial circumstance, it's time to actually speak with a mortgage loan professional. Prequalification is a simple process that will allow the mortgage professional to ascertain certain information for qualification purposes. Based on the information received (usually by phone), a prequalification letter can be completed for your use. The letter will give you and your realtor an indication of your buying power. This prequalification is only a preliminary scenario based on initial information provided. In the event that you are interested in a particular property, a prequalification letter gives you an advantage over other potential buyers who have not consulted with a mortgage professional first before writing a contract (which, by the way, is a terrible strategy). The letter will outline a possible loan amount, which will determine your maximum exposure, the loan term, loan program, and interest rate. You should retain a copy of the letter for your records and to use as a point of reference. It is important to remember that prequalification letters are based on initial overviews, and the numbers are not exact.

Information pertaining to your income will ultimately determine how much you can buy or how much of a loan you can be approved for. All figures found in your prequalification are preliminary and are considered "good," pending written verification of information provided.

In the prequalification process, there will be a review of your assets to determine the type of program you will qualify for. Additionally, an "in-file" credit report will indicate a snap shot of your credit profile. An in-file report is simply a rating given to your credit report based on the programs that are available to assist you in the buying process.

Obtaining a prequalification will help you when negotiating the contract for the home. The seller of the home may be more willing to work with you because you have a lender versus dealing with someone who may not have obtained the services of a mortgage professional regardless of how much money they bring to the table.

Another thing you should remember is that terms often change. For this reason, it is a good idea to revisit the terms and costs before executing a contract for a home that may cost more than your prequalification revealed.

Anyone looking to purchase a home for the first time or even repeat buyers should undoubtedly obtain a prequalification prior to beginning the search for a home. If you're wondering how soon you should consider beginning the prequalification process, I suggest at least 120 days before you desire to make a purchase. In the event that you are looking to buy at some point beyond the 120-day mark, call Equifax at 1-800-685-1111 to obtain a free copy of your credit report.

While it is important that you look early for a property, we don't recommend that you begin too early. When you find your home, you'll have to be ready to make a move fairly quickly. If you don't, you will find yourself frustrated because every home you desire will leave the market as fast as it was introduced.

Prequalification is important on a number of different levels. The process assists the mortgage company's ability to give you the most buying power possible. It also helps you determine the price range (and types of homes and neighborhoods) that best fits your property search. Your prequalification status also affirms that you can obtain the necessary financing to support your purchase. It also eliminates time at closing by indicating exactly what is needed to help you make the smoothest transition possible at the time of purchase.

If you've worked through the process and are dissatisfied with the qualified purchase price, the following will give you some suggestions to improve your mortgage amount.

### Analyze the Challenge

1. Are your debts too high? Do you have challenging credit? If you have too much challenging credit, you will need to take some time to reduce these debts and reestablish good credit. You'll then be in a better position to buy at a later date. If you owe less than ten months on any of your installment accounts, chances are that those monthly debt payments may be disregarded, which could help you to qualify for more home. Let your mortgage loan officer know if this is the case.

2. Is your income too low? (who would say no?) If your income is too low compared to your desired purchase price, you may need to wait until your income increases before you purchase a home. Do you anticipate that your household income will increase your earnings potential? If so, you may want to delay your purchase until proof of increased income can be verified. Another option is to consider a co-signer. Or if you've been working a part-time job for two years or more, that income can be used to determine your prequalification loan amount.

3. Are you being realistic? You may not be able to afford that dream house right now, but the fastest way to get it might

be to buy a less expensive starter home for now. If you live in it a while, take good care of it, and let it appreciate in value, you should be able to trade up at a later date.

Now, that you have gotten your prequalification, let's take it further and look at getting your preapproval.

# Chapter 8

---

*There is a difference between interest and commitment. When you're*
*interested in doing something, you do it only when it's convenient. When*
*you're committed to something, you accept no excuses, only results.*
Ken Blanchard
Author, *The One Minute Manager*

**Getting Your Preapproval**

Now that you have obtained your prequalification, it is now time
to get preapproved. In the preliminary stages of our search, your profile was based on information you provided verbally. The preapproval
is provided after having the information authenticated through written verification.

Prior to preapproval we must review all three credit scores from
the major reporting agencies. Not only is the credit score reviewed but
your credit pattern will also be looked at. Keep in mind that your credit
may be pulled for review one final time right before closing. I strongly
advise you not to apply for any new credit while going through the
process.

The purpose of preapproval is to give you a more definite approval determination. Unlike a prequalification, a preapproval is issued
based on a written verification of all assets, income, and credit. Additionally, the preapproval is more desirable than prequalification because it indicates that it has been officially reviewed and determined
that the loan request can be consummated.

Realtors and their sellers will perceive a preapproved homebuyer to be more prepared and stronger than a buyer who has simply been prequalified. In fact, you are two times more likely to be seriously considered as a potential buyer than having only a prequalification. In a seller's market, getting preapproval will allow you to move much faster through the lending process, and often time is critical.

With the advent of the Desktop Underwriter system, which replaces the process of having a person review your profile initially, preapproval can be obtained in a matter of minutes using this computer-generated program. It is not required to have a property address in order to obtain preapproval. Preapprovals are generally good for sixty days, considering there are no changes in your financial circumstances.

Preapprovals are usually obtained after the initial application. If there is a sense of urgency, a preapproval may be obtained the day of the initial call or prequalification. To eliminate an overwhelming amount of stress or minimize the potential for a frustrating buying experience, I recommend that you obtain preapproval as soon as possible. Preapproval adds a certain peace of mind for both yourself and all other parties involved, it affirms the program parameters, and it clarifies the financing required for down payments.

# Chapter 9

My brethren, count it all joy when you fall into divers temptations; knowing this, that the trying of your faith worketh patience. But let patience have her perfect work, that ye may be perfect and entire, wanting nothing.
James 1:3

**Processing Your Loan**

The processing of your loan is probably the most important part of the home-buying process. This is the time when all aspects of your application are verified. The goal is to minimize weaknesses and accentuate strengths. During this period you may be requested to update documents and/or explain things concerning your application.

Your loan application and all supporting documentation you supplied will form the basis of your loan package. Because so much money is at stake when lenders make mortgage loans, it is necessary for us to do a thorough investigation on the client to determine how risky your loan request may be. By the way, *every* loan is a risk to the lender.

Most mortgage companies cannot make a verbal commitment to approve your loan at the time of the interview. A decision on whether or not your loan will be approved is not made until all the verifications are completed. The verification process takes time, and this is when the waiting begins. Waiting to find out if your loan will be approved can be one of the most frustrating aspects of the entire home-buying process.

## Areas of Your Profile That Will Be Verified

### 1. Employment and Salary

Lenders will not just take your word for what kind of job you have or what your salary is. They will ask your employer for written verification on your current salary and your prospects for continued employment. You will also need to submit copies of your personal federal income tax returns for the previous two years.

### 2. Other Assets

The lender will want to know if you have any other source of income in addition to your salary. Other assets may include alimony or child support, social security, disability payments, savings accounts, trust funds, and stocks. All assets that you list will be verified by the lender.

### 3. Credit History

I also advised you to get a copy of your credit report before you apply for a loan so that you will have time to pay off delinquent accounts or correct mistakes on your report. Lenders will look at several things on your credit report:

a. Bankruptcy—If you claimed a bankruptcy, a credit letter, bankruptcy papers, and discharge will be required.

b. Debts—The lender will verify balances on charge cards and other installment or revolving charge accounts. If your debts are excessive, you may not be able to qualify.

c. Payment History—The lender will also look at how you've paid these accounts, whether or not you've paid them on time, and how often your payments have been late.

d. Rent Payments and Residential Stability—Your history of paying rent or mortgage payments is important because it indicates your commitment to pay for shelter. If you rent, the lender will verify the amount you pay for rent each month and the length of time you have lived at your present address. Your history of paying the rent will be particularly important if you pay cash for most of your purchases and do not have an active credit file.

### 4. The Property Appraisal

Lenders will ask for an appraisal on the house you wish to buy or refinance. The purpose of an appraisal is to determine the market value of the property. The appraised value tells the lender whether or not your offer is in line with what the house is worth. The appraisal serves as a protection for the lender and borrower.

### 5. Title Work

A title search is done to ensure that the seller is the legal owner of the property and that he or she is free to sell it. The title search also checks the title records to make sure that there are no liens on the title. Title insurance protects the loan in the event a flaw is discovered after the property has been bought.

### 6. Hazard Insurance Policy

Homeowners insurance or hazard insurance protects against loss in the event the house is damaged or destroyed by a disaster such as fire.

### Dos and Don'ts while Your Loan Is Being Processed

**Dos**
- Keep all accounts current (car payment, credit cards, etc.).
- Pay the difference of your current rent payment and your new mortgage payment to yourself in a separate account.

- Limit your spending to needs and forgo wants.
- Pay your rent on time.
- Stay organized (collect all bank statements and pay stubs to provide to your loan officer when needed).
- Keep copies of all paycheck stubs and any statements on bills being paid.
- Make rent payments by check or money order (if money order, keep copies of payments).
-

**Don'ts**
- Quit your job or get another job unless it is in the same line of work and for equal or more money.
- Allow anyone to make an inquiry on your credit report.
- Change bank accounts or transfer money within your existing bank accounts.
- Cosign for anyone.
- Purchase an auto or take on any additional debt.
- Purchase any other real estate.
- Apply for credit anywhere or complete any other credit applications.
- Charge any additional debt on any current credit card.

# Chapter 10

*If your ship doesn't come in, swim out to meet it.*
J. Winters, Actor

## Underwriting Your Loan

### The Four Cs of Final Approval

Once your loan profile has been processed and reviewed, the next step is for the processor to submit your file to underwriting. During the underwriting process, the four areas that will be verified are **Capacity, Capital, Collateral,** and **Credit.** The number one goal for the underwriter is to determine if your credit profile meets standards for the particular program you are applying for. There are three determinations that will result from underwriting review:

Approval—This usually will come with stipulations (conditions). Some stipulations include additional pay stubs, updated bank statements, and a credit letter of explanation.

Suspense—The underwriter may need additional information to render a decision. Usually in this instance there is something that isn't clear to the underwriter and will need further explanation in order to approve or deny.

Denial—Many times this denial should be construed as a delay. There may be some areas that will need work prior to getting a home loan.

### Capacity

Capacity is determined by your ability to sustain monthly mortgage payments and to maintain and manage your current creditor obligations. This is measured by a ratio termed **Debt to Income Ratio (DIR)** and is expressed as a percentage. This percentage will represent the amount of your income that will be used to pay your mortgage and all contractual bills. Key factors in getting an approval based on capacity are the front-end ratio and back-end ratio.

The **Front-end Ratio** compares your mortgage payment to your monthly income. For example, if your mortgage payment is $1,300, and your total *gross* monthly income is $3,000, your front-end ratio would be 43 percent. Forty-three percent of your income will be used to pay your mortgage payment. Usually lenders want your front end ratio to be 31%

$$\text{Debt } \frac{\$1,300}{\text{Income } \$3,000} = 43\%$$

The **Back-end Ratio** compares all monthly bill payments, including your new mortgage payment, to your total gross monthly income ($3,000). This is the most widely used ratio. For example, if your mortgage payment is $1,300 and you have other monthly bills totaling $450, your back-end ratio will be 58 percent. Fifty-eight percent of your income will be used to pay *all* of your contractual debts.

$$\text{Debt } \frac{\$1,750}{\text{Income } \$3,000} = 58\%$$

By using these standard ratios, underwriting will be answering these questions:

- Can you handle the monthly payments presented under your deed of trust?

- How does your new mortgage payment compare to your current rent payment?

- Will you be able to maintain timely payments on all of your other creditor accounts?

- Will you have money reserved for the unexpected?

There are three components that will affect your debt to income ratio:

- Your monthly Income
- Your monthly creditor payments
- The mortgage interest rate

**Monthly Income**

Underwriting usually doesn't look favorably on an applicant who has changed jobs several times in recent years. However, changing jobs should not be a problem if you have upgraded your job status or moved from one company to another to accept a better job. If you've held many different jobs in different fields (job hopping) within a short period, you may likely be considered a poor risk. Full-time income that will be accepted will be based on your gross monthly income (before taxes). If you plan to use part time income in determining your qualification, underwriting will need to verify that you've been getting overtime consistently over the past two years. Part-time income must be verified by pay stubs and W-2 forms.

Self-employed Individuals will have to produce two years of tax returns including all schedules. Income considered will be based on the net profit or loss of the company. In addition, income will be based on the percentage of the company that is owned by the borrower. For instance, if you have a 50 percent partner, the income used would be 50 percent of the net profit.

Other income that will be considered includes Social Security income, child support, disability income, and retirement income. All income will need proof that it will last for a minimum of three years.

**Creditor Payments**

Underwriting will verify your payments on contractual bills only. From an underwriting standpoint, certain debts are not counted, such as utility bills, insurance, and maintenance costs. Any installment loans, such as an automobile loan that you have less than ten months to pay on, will not be included in the debt ratio.

### Loan Program/Rate

The program and interest rate will have a direct impact on your debt to income ratio. The lower your rate, the lower your payment, which in turn will minimize your debt to income ratio. In addition, the longer your loan term (e.g., thirty or forty years), the better your debt ratios will be.

### Capital

Capital is used to describe on-hand cash used for **upfront costs, down payment, and closing costs**. There will be upfront money that is needed to get your home purchase started. The more money you have reserved for your purchase transaction, the better chance of your approval from underwriting. Let's take a moment to discuss in detail these costs.

**Upfront Cost.** These costs consist of the initial money needed to get the home-loan process completed. The following costs will be paid prior to going to settlement:

Credit Report
Earnest Money Deposit
Inspection
Appraisal
Homeowners Insurance

**Down Payment.** Your down payment represents money used to pay down on the purchase price of the home. There are a number of factors that will determine the down payment requirements:

Program—Some programs will allow for no money down.

Credit background—Your credit rating determines the type of program you can qualify for.

<u>Personal preference</u>—Some buyers will want to use their own money for the down payment.

**Down Payment Requirements**

As an example, the statutory down payment minimum for an FHA loan is 3.5 percent. This down payment can come from the use of savings, liquid assets, gifts, or a community program.

The following is a list of other sources that you may want to consider to come up with the upfront costs, the down payment, and the closing costs.

- Other liquid assets
- Stocks, bonds, thrifts, money markets
- Proceeds from sale of home
- Property trade-ins
- Employer
- Proceeds from a yard sale
- Gift from relative
- Cash in vacation
- Tax refund
- Increase exemptions
- 401(k) distribution
- IRA withdrawal
- Equity sharing
- Seller financing
- Local community crograms
- 

**Closing Costs**

Closing costs consist of the total sum that will be needed to close escrow. The closing-cost funds can come from the buyer, the seller, the lender, a community program, or a combination of these. The following are aspects of your loan that will have a direct impact on the amount needed for closing:

- Loan origination and points
- Interest rate
- Programs
- Property value
- Seller-paid closing costs

## Collateral

The second part to an approval will be verification of property value based on a certified real estate appraisal. Collateral is a term used to describe the property being secured under the terms of the deed of trust. The appraisal is the traditional ceremony of determining if you are paying too much for the property or to see if you are getting a good deal. Technically, the purpose of an appraisal is to protect the lender from loaning too much money on the property. The appraisal inspection lasts for approximately twenty to forty-five minutes, depending on the size of the home, identifiable physical problems, and the time of day.

The appraiser will ask questions, take measurements, and photograph exterior and interior parts of the house. The costs of appraisals are approximately $375 for a conventional appraisal and $500 for a FHA appraisal. The buyer has a right to receive a copy of the appraisal. Generally, if an appraisal for a property is too low (lower than the sales price), the lender may not approve the loan for the property. If the contract was contingent on a satisfactory appraisal, the buyer may be able to renegotiate the price down or get released from the contract.

There are two standard ways to appraise the value of a home and one uncommon method.

### Cost Approach

The cost approach is pretty straightforward. This method attempts to determine value by calculating how much it would cost today to build your home. The appraiser will measure the square footage of the home and multiply this number by cost-per-square-foot (determined by experience and means or a Marshall Swift report). Depreciation for age will be subtracted and lot value will be added (determined by assessment records). The end result will be the value by cost.

### Sales Approach

The sales approach compares houses of comparable size within the same neighborhood (usually within the past six months) within one mile, depending on availability and type of home. The appraiser will determine the square footage or the design and will need to make certain adjustments. Adjustments are made based on room count and amenities. Sales comparison analysis is determined and compares it to your sales contract to reach an indicated value by sales.

Most appraisal reports use both approaches to determine value to make a final determination. At the very bottom of the appraisal you will find the market value of your property. It is upon this that lenders typically base their loan terms.

### Income Approach

The income approach is more common in commercial real estate appraisal and in business appraisal. The fundamental math is similar to the methods used for financial valuation, securities analysis, or bond pricing. However, there are some significant and important modifications when used in real estate or business valuation.

### Home Inspection

A careful assessment of the physical condition of a house before purchase can save you time and money at a later date. Costly repairs to structural or mechanical systems can be avoided by a preliminary inspection of the property before a purchase offer is signed.

The buyer will usually have between five and ten days to complete an inspection.from the time of the contract being ratified. In certain instances, the contract can be contingent upon a completed inspection. An inspection is not usually required as a condition of your loan approval, however it is recommended. For certain community programs, however, an inspection may be required.

The normal areas that are inspected include the foundation, floors, walls, roof, windows and doors, plumbing, electrical system, heating and air conditioning, and energy efficiency. The cost of an inspection ranges from $200 to $600.

## Credit

*"Financial responsibility means being able to achieve your goals without sacrificing your future for instant pleasure"*
*Derick W. Hungerford*

Credit may be the most important of the Four Cs of approval. Money can come and money can go, but if you have good credit, you'll always be able to obtain funds when needed. I also think this subject is so very important because I've seen negative credit circumstances that could have been avoided. Those same issues have affected life's big decisions, such as buying a dream home. I often ask clients with very good credit how they managed to maintain such good credit. Invariably I get one of two answers: (1) their parent or an adult gave them advice about using credit or (2) they learned from a bad experience. (They either moved out of inspiration or desperation.)

My hope is to inspire you to want to aim for having the best credit possible. The bottom line is that credit cards and consumer debt can be a form of bondage. On the other hand, having access to credit lines and credit cards will have their purpose, if used with proper stewardship. I suggest that you count the cost before you buy. Simply being able to buy an item doesn't mean that you are equipped to afford that item. Keep in mind that there is an acquisition cost and a maintenance cost.

In addition, buying depreciable assets is one sure way of falling short of your financial goals. Credit may be one of the most important aspect of the approval process and definitely has the biggest impact on future costs. Debt can affect you for the rest of your life. My Episcopal pastor, John A. Cherry, often has said "credit cards are used for convenience and not for installment payments. You must have cash to pay the balance when the statement arrives."

I do however understand that people will sometimes have inescapable circumstances, but the biggest way to prevent this is to stay clear from having too much debt in the first place. There is a difference between good debt and bad debt. Examples of good debt include mortgage loans, investments, and even student loans. Examples of bad debts are credit cards, store charge cards, and car loans. The first thing you may want to do is divide your debt into good and bad categories. Credit can be good when you use it correctly, but conversely, it can be a person's worst nightmare if used inappropriately. But if you are going through a credit nightmare currently, it's not the end of the world. I've seen people recover from some very tough financial circumstances to go on to become successful and financially astute.

Here are some alarming statistics:

- The total current consumer credit is in the trillions of dollars.

- The average American has $9,400 in credit card debt.

- On average, Americans pay billions of dollars in total finance charges each year.

- Nearly 1.4 million credit card holders declared bankruptcy in 2012.

- Credit card debt has torn families apart. It has caused problems such as judgments and lawsuits for millions for people.

- Seventy percent of credit card holders can carry a balance from one month to another and can potentially carry a balance *forever* as long as they pay the minimum amount each month.

- Seven out of ten clients are turned down for a mortgage loan due to credit.

- Credit card companies send out nearly 2.5 billion offers for credit cards every year. (That is 10 offers for every man, woman, and child in America.)

**How Credit and Debt Can Affect Your Ability to Borrow**

It is important to understand how credit affects your ability to buy a home or borrow money. Your credit record demonstrates how you've handled credit in the past and how you currently pay your bills. Mortgage brokers and lenders use this information to determine whether you'll qualify for a loan. Your credit record can even affect the interest rate applied to the financing.

Many mortgage lenders are now using automated underwriting and credit-scoring systems to electronically accelerate the loan-approval process. In other words, in more and more instances, a computer is making the lending decision instead of a human being. This means there is less gray area in determining whether to lend you the money or not. It used to be that lenders would request, and ultimately accept, explanations for a late payment or a small collection. But that type of commonsense approach to lending is virtually on its way to extinction.

A credit score is a statistical way of predicting the likelihood that you, the borrower, will pay back a loan. Factors include individual records of repaying your mortgage, other loans and credit card bills, public records such as tax liens or bankruptcies, how often loans and credit cards are applied for, and how much is actually owed.

For example, those who charge up to the limit on credit cards may hurt their credits scores—even if they've never missed a payment in their entire credit history! Recent applications (also known as *inquiries*) for numerous cards, or for a car loan, even if unused, also may hurt credit scores. However, borrowers who show a pattern of managing credit wisely, such as keeping credit balances low and paying bills on time consistently, get positive marks.

## The Advent of the Desktop Underwriting

Until a few years ago, all of this information was evaluated manually by reviewing each piece of information separately, and it was very time consuming. Today, many lenders use a computer-based process to automate loan underwriting that evaluates the information easily, objectively, and often within minutes. This is why lenders find this decision-making processor so appealing. In addition to speeding up the loan process, automated credit scoring treats each person objectively without regard to race, religion, national origin, gender, or marital status. Credit scores are blind to demographic or cultural differences among loan applicants.

Of course on the flip side of that, credit scores are also blind to extenuating circumstances, forces of nature, job layoffs, putting three children through college, severe or chronic illnesses, etc. Credit scores can help lenders be fair so that no bias is given to a particular borrower, but unfortunately this type of lending process is still a double-edged sword.

While it may not be a good idea to have a lot of credit cards, or even a lot of "credit," it is important to use credit because it establishes a willingness to pay bills and establish a credit history. It's also a good idea to develop a savings habit and to pull back on consumer purchases to be in a better position to qualify for a mortgage or home equity loan.

The single most important thing you as a potential homebuyer or borrower can do is to pay your bills on time. At the very least, the minimum amount should be paid by the date it is due. Being late on a payment is a negative mark even if it is made up later. Even if you haven't paid your bills on time, you can start today because credit scores emphasize your most recent payment resources. Your credit file reports the previous seven years' history of your payment history. Public records like judgments, bankruptcies, and tax liens remain in your file for ten years. But a good repayment history in the last three years will be weighted greater in the credit-scoring process than poor history from six or seven years ago.

I urge you to check your credit records and make sure they're accurate. I've heard that over 30 percent of all credit reports have some type of error in them. Credit reports are made by three private companies:

| Equifax | Experian | Trans Union |
|---|---|---|
| 1-800-685-1111 | 1-800-682-7654 | 1-800-888-4213 |
| www.equifax.com | www.experian.com | www.transunion.com |

Credit records can vary from one of these companies to another, so you may wish to contact all three to resolve any potential problems in advance. There are modest fees for each report; however, if you are denied credit by anyone, you can get a free copy. There are also services that consolidate all three reports into one comprehensive document (for a nominal fee). One of them is Right to Know (www.righttoknow.com).

Any inaccuracies or disputed items must be investigated by the credit-reporting company within thirty days, and they must provide you with written notice of the results within five days of completion.

Building and maintaining good credit simply means improving your credit profile, paying bills on time, paying off outstanding debt, and limiting the amount of credit you use. Credit scores will improve over time through a pattern of positive credit use. Those with the lowest are in the 400s, but most individuals fall in the high 600 to low 700 range.

### The Purpose and Function of Credit Bureaus

The credit bureau has information from businesses and lenders reporting whether you pay your bills on time. The three major credit bureau agencies, Equifax, Trans Union, and Experian, are connected through a sophisticated, nationwide computer system. These organizations report information about your payment history on both your existing and previous debts. Each account is rated to indicate how you have repaid the obligation. Your credit report will contain a credit score. The purpose of the credit bureau system is to help businesses decide whether or not to grant the applicant credit. It is important to understand that credit bureaus do not make the decision to grant your request for credit. They merely provide information from their records concerning your credit history to the lender requesting that information.

### What's with the FICO Scores (Credit Score)?

Your FICO scores are determined by a mixture of five parts:

**1. Your payment history (35%):** This includes accounts in collection—whether you have any delinquencies and how frequent and recent they are—and your score depends on whether the other information in the rest of your history is good because the model looks at credit patterns, not isolated credit mistakes.

**2. The amount of outstanding debt (30%):** FICO considers the number of balances recently reported—the average balances compared to credit limit. Having balances near your maximum limit is held against you and will affect your score even if you consistently pay the minimum payment each month on time.

**3. Your credit history (15%):** FICO looks at how long you have had your account, the total number of inquiries and new accounts opened, and the amount of time since the most recent inquiry. Statistics show that those anticipating financial troubles try to increase the number of credit lines they have available. FICO models treat all inquiries occurring with a fourteen-day period as one inquiry. All models will ignore car- and mortgage-related inquires that occur within a thirty-day period before calculating your score.

**4. The types of credit you use (10%):** FICO looks at the diversity of credit you use—bank cards, travel and entertainment cards, department store cards, personal finance company references, and/or installment loans.

**5. Negative information (10%):** This includes bankruptcies, delinquencies, or late payments on accounts, collections, too many credit lines with maximum available funds borrowed, and/or too little credit history (less than five credit lines in the past two years)

### Information FICO Does Not Consider

FICO does not consider race, color, religion, national origin, sex, marital status, age, job, or profession.

### What Is a Good Credit Score?

Credit scoring requires that you have at least one account that is older than six months and have at least one account that has been reported to the credit bureau in the last six months (this could be the same account). If the score on a borrower's credit report is too low for one program, it may be acceptable for other products. Borrowers with a score below 620 may find it a little difficult getting the best loan rates and terms or may have to put up a larger down payment.

| | |
|---|---|
| Below 620 | = Cautious Review (Problem) |
| 620–660 | = Comprehensive Review (Fair) |
| 660–700 | = Basic Review (Good) |
| 700 or above | = Minimal Review (Excellent) |

## How Can I Improve My Credit Score?

Keep in mind that as negative information ages, it has less importance. Getting back on track usually takes one full year of responsible payment in your credit report, conservative use of credit, paying on time, and not requesting too much credit during a short period of time.

### Correct Errors

You should get a copy of your credit report and make sure all of your information is complete and accurate. Remember that removing or changing one incorrect derogatory item from your credit report will not guarantee an increase in the score.

### Keep Inquiries to a Minimum

Keeping inquiries at a minimum (below five per year) will help your credit score. Applying for multiple credit cards, consumer loans, car loans, etc., will have an adverse affect on your report score.

### Close Some of Your Accounts

Close unneeded accounts. In some cases, the less available credit you have, the less risk you will pose to a mortgage lender. To build your credit and improve your scores, keep around two to four credit cards for the best score.

Just cutting up your cards and throwing them away does not close your credit card account. The best way to close a credit card account is by sending a certified letter to the customer service department. Ask the credit card company to close your account and to report your account to credit bureaus as "closed by consumer." Closing accounts are for borrowers who have a lot of available credit; however, in general, leaving credit cards open and using them will help to increase your score.

**Pay Down Credit Cards**

Conservative use of credit is important—keep balances at below 30 percent of the available credit for credit cards.

**Pay Credit Obligations on Time**

The longer history you have of responsibly using credit and paying on time, the better your score.

**The Danger of Credit Cards**

Buying on credit used to occur directly between the buyer and the seller. Credit cards became popular in the 1960s, and now using this intermediate plastic agent called a credit card is as normal as using a cell phone The difference between now and then is that almost everyone paid his or her balances off at the end of the month. It was considered unwise to carry debt. Today credit cards are not only encouraged but also have been perpetrated as a sign of prestige. They have become so pervasive that credit card companies have contracted with colleges and universities to offer young adult college students credit cards as early as freshmen year. In my opinion there should be a law against these egregious acts.

## Watch for These Credit Card Tricks

**1. Tricky teaser rates**—Teaser rates don't last. But they are very tempting, especially if you are looking to transfer an existing balance from one credit card to another. Before you sign up for a card with a low interest rate, find out what that rate applies to. New purchases, cash advances, balance transfers?

**2. Pursuing the un-creditworthy**—Creditors often prey on those who are least creditworthy by scanning credit records for signs of financial trouble. If you are a student with no income or have recently emerged from bankruptcy, beware, credit card companies will try to contact you. Keep in mind that your terms will be very unfavorable.

**3. The magically appearing annual fee**—You signed up for a card with no annual fee. Then out of the blue, you find one. Some lenders start charging an annual fee to their customers who pay their bill off every month; cancel that card.

**4. A sliding credit line**—Some lenders entice customers to use a cash advance check or to skip a month's payment and then lower their credit limit. The maxed-out customer is then charged an additional fee for being above the limit.

**5. Mysterious fees**—Transactional fees are charged for calling the toll-free number to check out balances and penalty fees are charged for account inactivity.

**6. The disappearing grace period**—Some lenders will pull the grace period out from under you—especially if you pay the balance in full every month. If your grace period is eliminated, you'll accrue interest from the day you make a purchase. The only way to avoid a finance charge would be to pay your bill before you receive it.

## How to Build a Good Record

- Open a checking account or savings account, or both. Use checks to pay your bills. Cancelled checks can be used to show you pay utility bills or rent regularly, which is a sign of reliability.

- Ask your bank if you may deposit funds with a financial institution to serve as collateral for a credit card (secured credit card).

- If you are new in town, request a summary of any credit record kept by a credit bureau in your former town. Ask the bank or department store in your old hometown for the name of the agency it reports to.

- (Normally, I would not suggest co-signing for anyone. However, if you do have someone who will offer to co-sign, please make sure you pay your debt on time and be a good steward; someone has trusted you with their name)

- If you don't qualify on the basis of your own credit standing, seek someone to cosign for you.

- If you are turned down, find out why and try to clear up misunderstandings (before applying for an additional credit card).

## What to Do before Buying a Home

There are a few things related to credit that you may want to implement before you purchase your home:

- Defer major expenses until after you have closed on your home.

- Do not take on more credit before closing on your home.

- Pay down other consumer debt to reduce monthly payments.

- Consolidate bills to obtain lower monthly costs (be wary of transfer fees when consolidating).

- When possible, switch from high-cost credit cards to cards with lower interest rates. Be careful of higher future rates and transfer costs.

**How to Solve Credit Problems**

There are no quick fixes to a poor credit history. Your financial future depends on your ability to plan and control your use of credit, and that will require time and commitment.

- Contact each creditor personally and explain your situation. Let your creditors know that you are concerned and that you want to work out a realistic plan to repay your debts. Making good-faith payments can help. If you don't have the money or you don't plan to fulfill your end of the bargain, don't make empty promises.

- If your credit report shows a pattern of late payments that are associated with specific problems such as a sudden illness or the loss of your job, you can write a letter of explanation.

- If you have outstanding collections or judgments against you, take steps to pay them off. Contact the creditors and begin making regular payments, or payoff in full if you are able.

- If you cosigned a loan for a car and the payments are not made, the late payment will remain on both credit reports. You will continue to be held responsible for this debt until it is repaid.

- Maintain all documentation from all paid accounts, and obtain paid-in-full verification.

- Do not go to credit repair shops—unless you have a dependable reference.

- Try to solve credit problems without filing for bankruptcy if at all possible.

- If a family crisis or loss of income has caused a problem more serious than you can deal with by yourself, contact the nearest nonprofit credit counseling service.

**Getting Out of Debt**

Being in debt is both a financial condition and a state of mind.

Financial responsibility means being able to achieve your goals without sacrificing your future for instant pleasure. When you put yourself in debt, you are selling a part of your future for products or services you may have purchased recently. You may have to take a part-time job that you don't enjoy because you have entered into a deal to swap future earning for a new TV, car, clothing, or dinner out. If you immediately stop doing the things that got you into debt, you won't put yourself any further in debt. My advice would be to stop impulse buying! The ultimate goal of being debt free is much more rewarding than the feeling you get when buying a new flat-screen TV. By simply writing down your expenses and reviewing the list, you can immediately cut out some of your unnecessary spending. At the end of the month you can break down your spending into categories and add up the individual items to find out exactly how much you spent in each area. Review your previous months' spending and cut back in the areas where you are able. Write down your plan (achievable goals) for becoming debt free and read it often. (see workbook for budget sheet)

**Six Steps to Eliminating Credit Card Debt**

Unpaid credit card balances are the worst kind of debt. Organize a plan for paying these off, and make it a priority. A goal may be to carry only one or two credit cards and pay balances off at the end of each month.

1. Stop using your cards. The last thing you want to do is to add to your present heavy debt load. Take all your credit cards out of your wallet and leave them at home, or better yet, cancel them if that's what it takes. Keep one for emergency purposes.

2. Stop the flood of credit card offers. You can force credit bureaus to stop selling your name and address. Dial 1-888-5-OPTOUT to get your name removed from mailing.

3. Always pay more than the minimum. The credit card companies are just being nice (yeah, right) when they require only a small minimum payment of your total balance. They calculate this minimum to extend your payments as long as possible to boost their profits. Pay as much as you can above the minimum *every* month.

4. Plan your attack. Don't just throw yourself at a mountain of debt without a plan or preparation. How many cards do you have? What interest rate do they charge? Which have the highest balance? Write down your card balances and the interest rates. Generally you'll want to start paying off the cards with the highest payment first, and then the next highest, and so on.

5. Reduce the interest rate. Most credit cards charge anywhere from 16 to 20 percent. You may be able to negotiate with your credit card company for a lower rate, particularly if you've had any of your cards for a while. This may be an advantage of being a faithful customer. Call them up to demand a lower rate and let them know that you are shopping around.

6. Consider combining your debts onto two of your lowest-rate cards if you have credit room available. (If you're maxed out on all your cards, this won't be an option.)

If you're making payments above the minimum, have reduced the interest rates on your cards, and have consolidated your debt, then you're in a better position with your credit card debt.

## How Many Credit Cards Are Enough?

In the end, your goal is to carry only one or two credit cards (if you have completed building and improving your credit), and pay off the balances each month. If you've gotten carried away and have five or six credit cards, consider the benefits of closing out most of them. Fewer cards will be easier to track. In addition, you'll have a much better sense of your overall debt level when it's on one or two rather than spread across a bunch of them.

You'll want to have at least one credit card to build your credit history. If you are married, your spouse should have one card in his or her name only for the same reason. If you can not trust yourself, too many cards can hurt your credit rating, particularly if they all have large unpaid balances. There should also be a spending limit for both credit cards. The more cards you have, the easier it is to get caught up in excessive spending. The fewer cards with the lowest balances are the best way to take control.

## Protection Laws

## Consumer Credit Protection Act of 1968

The Consumer Credit Protection Act required, for the first time, to state the cost of borrowing in a common language so that you the customer could figure out exactly what the charges would be, compare costs, and shop around for the credit deal best for you. This law indicates that you cannot be turned down for a credit card just because, for instance, you're a single woman; that you can limit your risk if a credit card is lost or stolen; that you can straighten out errors in your monthly bill without damage to your credit rating; and that you won't find credit shut off just because you've reached the age of sixty-five.

## Truth in Lending and Consumer Leasing Acts

The Truth in Lending Act requires creditors to give you certain basic information about the cost of buying on credit or taking out a loan. These disclosures can help you shop around for the best deal. If any creditor fails to disclose information required under these acts, or gives inaccurate information, or does not comply with the rules about credit or the right to cancel certain home-secured loans, you can sue for twice the finance charge in the case of payments.

### Equal Credit Opportunity Act

Discrimination based on age, color, race, religion is illegal. If you think you can prove that a creditor has discriminated against you for any reason, you may have a case for punitive damages.

### Fair Credit Billing Act

A creditor who breaks the rules for the correction of billing errors automatically loses the amount owed on the item in question, and any finance charges on it, up to a combined total of $50—even if the bill was correct. Billing errors also include errors in arithmetic; failure to show a payment or other credit to your account; failure to mail the bill to your current address (if you told the creditor about an address change at least twenty days before the end of billing period); and questionable items or an item for which you need more information.

### In Case of Error

If you discover an error, notify the creditor in writing within sixty days after the bill was received. Be sure to write to the address the creditor lists for billing inquiries and indicate for them to pay all parts of the bill that are not in dispute. While waiting for an answer, you do not have to pay the amount in question (the disputed amount) or any minimum payments or finance charges that apply. If the creditor made a mistake, you do not pay any finance charges on the disputed amount. Your account must be corrected, and you must be sent an explanation of any amount you still owe. If no error is found, the creditor must send you an explanation of the reasons for that finding and promptly send a statement of explanation.

## Defective Goods or Services

Your new sofa arrives with only three legs. You try to return it without success. You ask the merchant to repair or replace it; still no success. The Fair Credit Billing act allows you to withhold payment on any damaged or poor quality goods or services purchased with a credit card, as long as you have made a real attempt to solve the problem with the merchant.

This right may be limited if the card was a bank, travel, or entertainment card, or any card not issued by the store where you made your purchase. In such cases, the sale must have been for more than $50 and must have taken place in your home state or within one hundred miles of your home

## Credit Repair Organizations Act

Credit records will sooner or later affect your lifestyle in several areas. Factual information on bad debts stays on your record. The Credit Repair Organizations Act bars credit repair companies from taking money up front, mandates that they inform you of your legal rights, and says they must spell out the terms of their contract. The act also prohibits a variety of false and misleading statements as well as fraud by credit repair organizations receiving payment before any promised service is fully performed. Services must be under written contract, which must include a detailed description of the services and contract-performance time. Organizations must provide the consumer with a separate written disclosure statement describing the consumer's right before entering into the contract.

## Student Loans

Over the years many of my clients' student loan payments have affected their debt ratios and credit rating. Here are a few pointers about student loans.

There are three basic payment plans:

1. Standard Repayment Plan

With a standard plan, you usually pay the same amount each month for ten years. Standard repayment plans come with the highest monthly payments but cost the least in the long run because the loans are paid off the quickest.

2. Graduated Repayment Plan

Under a graduated plan, your payments start out low and increase every few years. This is often the best option for people just starting a career or business that have a low income that's likely to increase over time. If you qualify for the graduated plan, your payments start at as little as one half of what they would be under the standard plan and then increase every few years.

3. Extended Repayment Plan

Under an extended repayment plan, each year your monthly payments are recalculated based on your prior year's annual income, household income, and loan amount. The amount you pay annually will never exceed 20 percent of your discretionary income. To qualify for an income contingent plan, you must authorize the IRS to release your income information to the Department of Education.

As of October 7, 1998, all student loans are non-dischargeable in Chapters 7 and 13 Bankruptcies, except under the "undue hardship" provision, which is extremely difficult to show.

A loan generally defaults when payment has not been made for more than 180 days, and no payment arrangements have been worked out with the lender. If you are having challenges making full payments or timely payments, you may have some options.

## Option I

<u>Loan Consolidation</u>

With loan consolidation, you can lower your monthly payments by combining several loans into one packaged loan. Most consolidation lenders won't accept your application unless you have an outstanding balance of at least $7,500 on your eligible loans. All consolidation lenders allow you to stretch the term of your loan to anywhere from twelve to thirty years, depending on your balance.

## Option II

<u>Postponing Payments</u>

If you can't cancel your student loans, you can probably find a way to postpone making payments by obtaining a deferment or forbearance.

A ***deferment*** is a delay based on a specific condition, such as returning to school or being unemployed. This excuses you from making payments for a set period of time.

**Unemployment**. You can defer the payments on most loans, usually for up to three years if you are unemployed but looking for work.

**Economic hardship**. You can defer payments on federal loans obtained after June 30, 1993, for up to three years if you are suffering an economic hardship. You are automatically entitled if you receive public assistance.

**Enrollment in school**. If you return to school to study at least half time, you can almost always defer the payments on your student loans.

A *forbearance* is permission from your loan holder to stop making payments for a set period of time. Forbearances are easier to obtain than deferments because they are not tied to the type of loans you have or the date you obtained them, but they cost more (due to interest accrual).

**Option III**

Canceling Your Loans

If you've considered all repayment options and you still can't pay, there still are options. In certain limited circumstances, you may be able to cancel your student loans.

**In the event of death.** Well I guess someone will have the option of canceling your loan for you.

**Temporary or total disability.** A temporary or permanent disability will allow you to be eligible to apply for a cancellation.

**Membership in a uniformed service**. If you currently serve the U.S. government in the U.S. military, the National Oceanic and Atmospheric Corps, or the U.S. Public Health Service, there are several situations in which you may cancel or defer your loans.

**Performing community service**. In many situations you can partially cancel your student loans or defer your payments in exchange for performing community service. The Peace Corps or volunteering your time with an organization that assists low-income people in your community are two options.

**Bankruptcy**

Bankruptcy filing will put into place what is called an *automatic stay*, which stops virtually any of your creditors from attempting to collect debts.

If your financial situation has not changed for the better, there are two types of consumer bankruptcies that you may consider. My counsel is that bankruptcy should be your last resort.

## Chapter 7

Chapter 7 is essentially a liquidation case where your nonessential property may be sold to pay off your creditors. If you're behind on your mortgage and you file for Chapter 7 bankruptcy, the foreclosure may be stopped only temporarily. You cannot make up back payments in Chapter 7 or try to get back on track with your mortgage. Instead, the lender will probably ask that the automatic stay be lifted so that it can proceed with the foreclosure. The bankruptcy court will probably grant the request. The court exercises its control through a court-appointed person called a *bankruptcy trustee*. The trustee's primary duty is to see that your creditors are paid as much as possible. Chapter 7 bankruptcies are sometimes called *straight* bankruptcy. It cancels all or most of your debts; in exchange, you might have to surrender some property. You will complete paperwork describing your property, income, monthly living expenses, debts, exempt property (the property you keep through bankruptcy), and any property you sold or gave and money you spent. The trustee presents your papers at a short creditors' meeting.

A bankruptcy judge who decides you have enough assets or income to repay your debts can dismiss your Chapter 7 bankruptcy case or convert it to a Chapter 13 filing.

Bankruptcy is geared toward the honest debtor who got too deep in debt and simply needs the help of a bankruptcy court. Engaging in any questionable activities, such as transferring assets to friends or relatives to hide them from creditors, incurring debts for non-necessities when you reported that you were broke, or misleading the trustee about your income or debts on a credit application, can be the basis for your case being thrown out.

In addition, if you've recently run up large debts for a vacation, hobby, or entertainment, filing for bankruptcy probably won't help you. Most luxury debts incurred just before filing are not dischargeable if the creditor objects.

**Will Chapter 7 Discharge Enough of your Debts?**

Certain debts cannot be discharge in Chapter 7 bankruptcies:

- Back child support and alimony
- Student loans that began after 1993
- Income taxes less than three years past due
- Debts incurred on the basis of fraud, such as dishonesty on a credit application
- Debts from willful or malicious injury to another or another's property
- Debts from larceny (theft), breach of trust, or embezzlement
- Debts you are obligated to pay under a divorce settlement

**Chapter 13**

Chapter 13 is a reorganization bankruptcy. You must have disposable income for repayment. You are allowed to make up your mortgage arrears as a part of your plan as long as you immediately begin to make the regular payments called for in your contract. If you can't make at least the regular payment presently, a Chapter 13 bankruptcy might not be able to help you keep your home.

Situations that may make a good candidate for Chapter 13 bankruptcy include

- You are behind on your mortgage or car loan and want to make up the missed payments and reinstate the original agreement. You can achieve this goal through a Chapter 13 bankruptcy.

- You owe federal income taxes. Unless you meet several conditions, you cannot discharge federal income taxes in Chapter 7 bankruptcy. You can use Chapter 13 bankruptcy to pay the IRS over time.

- You have property you'd lose if you filed Chapter 7 bankruptcy.

- You received a Chapter 7 discharge within the previous six years.

- You have a co-debtor on a personal debt.

- You have a sincere desire to repay your debts, but you need the protection of the bankruptcy court to do so.

## Eligibility Requirements of Chapter 13 Bankruptcies

You will not qualify for Chapter 13 bankruptcy if your secured debts exceed $750,000. Home loans and car loans are common examples of secured debts. In addition, your unsecured debts cannot exceed $250,000.

A requirement is that the claimant must have steady income that is likely to continue.

Also the claimant must have disposable income. To determine if your disposable income is high enough, you must create a monthly budget. If the trustee or a creditor thinks your budget includes expenses other than necessities, it may be challenged.

## How to Avoid Bankruptcy Altogether

Although bankruptcy seems to be an easy solution to financial problems, it can be quite painful and carries consequences for years. Laws have been changed, making it a little more difficult to claim bankruptcy. Your bankruptcy will be listed on your credit report for up to ten years, even if you filed but was later dismissed or withdrawn.

Bankruptcy should be a last choice in rectifying your credit situations. Suggestions for avoiding bankruptcy include

- Organize a realistic spending plan.
- Be a wise shopper.
- Cut as many expenses as possible.
- Get medical insurance.
- Don't carry credit card balances.
- Avoid large rent or house payments.
- Don't cosign a loan for someone.
- Don't join finances with someone who has questionable spending habits.
- Don't put all of your money into high-risk investments.
- Periodically get a copy of your credit report.
- When going through financial difficulty, don't apply for more credit.
- Get help before your situation becomes uncontrollable.

# Chapter 11

*For which of you wanting to build, sit down not first to count the cost,*
*whether you have enough to finish it or not,*
Luke 14:28

## Counting the Costs of Home Stewardship

There are essentially four cost categories that you will need to consider as you pursue home stewardship.

*Upfront Costs*—All costs associated with holding a property for consideration and getting your mortgage loan approved and funded

*Down Payment*—Costs to meet the minimum deposit on the home purchase

*Closing Costs*—Money needed to pay all parties to settle the transaction

*Periodic Costs*—Monthly carrying costs consisting of your principle, interest, taxes, and insurance payment

There will be upfront costs that should be prepared for prior to closing. These costs are spread out over a period of time that ranges from the time of the initial offer to a couple of days prior to settlement.

**Upfront Costs**

| | |
|---|---|
| Credit report | $15–$25 |
| EMD (earnest money deposit) | $1,000–$2,000 |
| Inspection | $300–$600 |
| Appraisal | $375–$425 |
| Homeowners insurance | $500–$800 |

**The two major cost of buying a home will be your down payment and your closing costs.**

## Down Payment Costs

| | |
|---|---|
| FHA Loan | 3.5 percent down |
| Conventional Loan | 10 percent down |
| VA Loan | 0 percent down |
| USDA | 0 percent down |

### Example: $100,000 Purchase Price

| | |
|---|---|
| FHA Down Payment | $3,500 |
| Conventional Down Payment | $10,000 |
| VA Loan Down Payment | $0 |
| USDA Down Payment | $0 |

## Closing Costs

| | |
|---|---|
| FHA Loan | 5–6 percent of purchase price |
| Conventional Loan | 5–6 percent of purchase price |
| VA Loan | 5–6 percent of purchase price |
| USDA | 5–6 percent of purchase price |

Example: $100,000 purchase price
Closing costs = $5,000—$6000

## The Periodic Costs of a Home

In addition, there are other costs associated with home ownership – upkeep, gas bill, water bill, electric bill, repairs, etc. According to your deed of trust, you will be liable for making a monthly payment in order to pay off your loan within a specified term. The term of a mortgage simply refers to the number of years you have to repay the loan—for instance 15, 20, or 30 years. The mortgage term will greatly impact the monthly mortgage payment, since the longer the term, the less each monthly payment will be.

**PITI**—This is an acronym that refers to four components of a monthly mortgage payment.

P—Principal
I—Interest
T—Taxes
I—Insurance

PITI is used by the lender to compute the ratio of housing expenses to income in order to determine whether you can afford the mortgage. The tax and insurance amounts are paid monthly, to be held in an escrow account on your behalf so that the lender can pay them as they become due.

Generally, a lender will want your monthly mortgage payment to total no more than 31 percent of your monthly gross income (that's your monthly income before taxes and other paycheck deductions are taken out).

**Monthly Income**—Monthly income refers to the "gross" (before taxes) amount of income you receive each month. If you are paid an annual salary, this number will represent your salary divided by twelve months.

For example, if your annual salary is $36,000 a year, your monthly gross income is $3,000 ($36,000 divided by twelve months). If you are paid on an hourly basis and work forty hours a week, your gross monthly income is computed by multiplying your hourly rate by 2,080 hours (forty hours a week over fifty-two weeks) and then dividing by twelve months. For example, if your hourly rate is $10 an hour, your monthly gross income would be equal to $10 X 2,080 divided by 12 = $1,733.33. The lender will use your gross monthly income to determine whether you can support the mortgage payments. (see work book)

**Loan Limits**—The maximum amount of money you can borrow to purchase a home will vary depending on the mortgage product you choose. Conventional loan limits are established for loans that conform to guidelines established by Fannie Mae and Freddie Mac. There are limits on loans that exceed these limits or nonconforming loans (often called jumbo loans), as established by individual lenders. For FHA loans, maximum lending limits have been established for each area of the country.

**Qualifying Ratios**—As part of the qualifying process, the lender will use ratio calculations to determine whether you have enough stable income to support the monthly mortgage payment you'll be making. These calculations are often referred to as debt-to-income ratios. There are two ratio calculations performed by the lender: one to determine the housing debt-to-income ratio (or top/front ratio) and another to determine the total monthly debt-to-income ratio (or bottom/back ratio).

The housing debt-to-income ratio can vary from 28 percent to 31 percent.
The total monthly debt-to-income can range from 36 percent to 44 percent. ( higher ratios are accepted in certain cases i.e high credit scores, large amount of assets)

To compute the total monthly debt ratio (bottom/back), the lender will divide the total monthly debt, including PITI, by your gross monthly income. Please note that Self employed buyers will be qualified slightly differently than W-2 Waged employees.  With self employed individuals, lenders will use "net" income as opposed to "gross" income for wage earners.  Many times, income for the self employed will be calculated by using the 'net profit/loss' from 1040 tax returns.

Monthly Mortgage Payment / Gross Monthly Income

To compute the total monthly debt ratio (bottom/back), the lender will divide the total monthly debt, including PITI, by your gross monthly income.

Monthly Mortgage Payment + Bills / Gross Monthly Bills

The following four key factors are used by lenders to determine whether you can qualify for a mortgage loan:

**Income Stability**—To find out the potential stability of the borrower's income, in most cases, the lending institution will send a Verification of Employment (VOE) to the borrower's employer, collect updated pay stubs, and review W-2 and tax returns for the previous two years.

**Enough Income**—Lenders assess their risk by determining whether the borrower has enough stable income to support the mortgage payment along with the borrower's other financial obligations.

**Money to Close**—Another key factor lenders consider is the source and amount of funds the borrower has available to close escrow.

**Ernest Money**—A minimum investment of earnest money (or consideration) is required on nearly all home purchases. This deposit is usually due at the time of contract offer and will represent an average of 1 percent of the purchase price.

The probability of you being employed with a steady income throughout the course of your loan is very important to the lender. The Verification of Employment (VOE) determines the start date of employment, position, title, the current year to date and previous year's salary, any bonus or overtime paid on a regular basis, and the probability of continued employment. To ensure this form is not tampered with, it must be sent by the lender directly to the employer.

**The Breakdown of Your Cost:**

**Down Payment = 3.5 percent (for FHA)**

**Closing Costs = <u>6.0 percent</u>**

**Total Cost = 9.5 percent**

**You will need a total of 9.5 percent, which can partially come from:**

## 1) The seller
## 2) Down payment assistance program

## and

## 3) YOU!

# Chapter 12

**Understanding the Terms of Your Loan**

As a new home steward, it's imperative that you understand the terms of your loan. The current state of the housing market (although as a buyer you may be benefiting) is a result of all parties involved in the process, ranging from Wall Street investors to the consumer. The mortgage market has gone through turbulent times, and now more than ever before it's important that you get the best education, advice, and direction as you pursue your goal. Because your home will likely be the biggest asset and biggest debt you will ever have, it's extremely important to understand the terms of your mortgage loan. I suspect that many people who suffered through foreclosure did not understand the terms of their loan. My desire is for you to be a successful home steward. There is no sense in buying a home if you won't be able to keep the home. Knowing the specifics about your individual loan will help put you in a successful situation.

When structured properly, your house can be the centerpiece of your wealth-building strategy. There are mortgage programs that are good, and there are many that may not fit your strategy. Choosing the right tool is the key in having a successful mortgage. For instance, adjustable-rate mortgages increase over time and may not be the correct tool for some homeowners. A strategy that takes into consideration the time you'll be living in the home, income projections, and retirement needs plays a very critical role in determining which mortgage is right for you. With the recent challenges in the mortgage industry, it's important now to have a trusted mortgage advisor who can help you navigate through today's mortgage maze. Today, a mortgage is not just a home loan, but instead a strategic instrument that must be tied into your long- and short-term personal financial plan. Getting a mortgage likely involves far more money than any other financial decision you will be involved with, and many people have gone about it the wrong way, costing themselves thousands of dollars in lost opportunity.

**Please take time to know the following:**

### When are your monthly payments due?

When I ask this question, I sometimes get "the fifteenth" as an answer. Your payment is due on the first of each month. The lender usually allows you to have a grace period of fifteen days. However, your payment technically is due on the first. Read your paperwork to confirm your payment due date.

### How many years is your mortgage loan amortized over?

Make sure you know how many years it will take you to pay off your home loan. Do you have a thirty- or fifteen-year loan? Is your note a balloon? You can get all of this information from your note.

### What is your total monthly payment?

Your payment will consist of five parts: principle, interest, taxes, insurance, and mortgage insurance. If you have to pay a HOA or condo fee, these monthly cost will be paid separately.

### Is your mortgage escrowed?

Having your taxes and insurance included in your mortgage payment may be a good idea if you are a first-time home buyer. Be sure to confirm that these costs are included in your total payment.

### Are you paying mortgage insurance?

More than likely, you will pay mortgage insurance, especially if you are financing your home loan with a FHA loan. However, it is a good idea to know the exact monthly cost of the mortgage insurance and approximately how long you will be required to pay.

### What is your interest rate? APR?

It's extremely important to know what your note rate is. In addition, knowing your APR may be a little helpful so you are able to understand what you are paying as an annualized figure. This allows you to compare costs.

### Do you have a fixed or an adjustable rate?

Making sure your loan doesn't have a ticking time bomb is very important. If you desire to have a fixed rate, make sure you confirm that your rate will not adjust at any time during the term of your loan.

### Do you have a prepayment penalty?

Although most loans these days do not have a prepayment penalty, it's important that you make sure your loan documents do not contain such language. A prepayment penalty requires you to pay an additional amount of money in the event that you pay off your loan prior to the term date.

### What is your total yearly property tax payment?

Your property tax may fluctuate from time to time. Make sure to know your total yearly tax payment liability.

## How much is your yearly homeowners insurance premium?

Similarly to your property tax liability, it is wise to know what you are paying yearly for your homeowners insurance policy.

## Are there any special repayment requirements for assistance programs?

Usually down payment assistance programs require you to live in your home for a certain amount of years. Penalties are usually assessed if you sell or refinance your home prior to that term limit.

## Will the company bill you or will you receive a payment coupon?

You should be able to get this information at the time of closing. Usually your lender will have an initial payment coupon at closing.

## Are there any other special assessments for the home?

Make sure you are aware of any special assessments for your property. Also confirm the amount due per month for condo fees or HOA fees. Be sure to confirm the amount due per month for condo fees or HOA fees. In addition, make sure you are aware of any special assessments for your property such as a front foot water bill, special tax assessments, etc. Inquire with the settlement attorney to make sure you are aware of any additional monthly cost. Also, Homeowners Insurance DOES NOT cover flood damage and if your property is located in a "flood zone" you may be required to pay an additional premium for flood coverage. In addition, you may want to make sure you have replacement cost covered under your Homeowners Insurance Policy for building and personal property.

# Chapter 13

*There is a secret psychology to money. Most people don't know about it. That's why most people never become financially successful. A lack of money is not the problem; it is merely a symptom of what's going on inside you.*
T. Harve Eker
Author and motivational speaker

## Equity Benefits of Home Stewardship

Equity is the difference between what you owe (remaining balance of the mortgage loan) and the value of the home (the appraisal value). Unlike when you are renting, every time you make a monthly payment, you build equity in the home. Should you decide to sell the home, the equity (total amount of monthly payments and appreciation) has created a cash reserve account for you to access. Two factors have a direct impact on your equity: **loan reduction** and **appreciation**. As you make monthly payments, the difference between your balance and the value increase. In addition, the natural home appreciation in your area will further increase the value of your equity.

Your equity appreciates (increases in value) in a number of ways. As the cost of goods and services increases, the inflation rate rises, which makes the value of your home go up as well. Supply deals with the availability of property. Keep in mind, when there is an increase in the supply of homes (decrease in demand or fewer buyers), housing prices will fall. This can be affected by the labor force, construction costs, and government monetary policies. Demand refers to the desirability of a property, which can be linked to the appreciation value of your home. This can also be linked to the overall population, demographics, employment, and wage levels as well. When there is a need for housing (demand increase), housing values (equity) will rise. In other words the fewer homes on the market, the more buyers will be scrambling to offer contracts. This decrease in the amount of homes available will cause prices to increase. Conversely, when there are a myriad of homes available, buyers then have more options. When options are available, prices go down.

Owning a home is a major source of savings for the average American household. Equity can also be used to pay college expenses and other immediate or pressing needs. Nationally, the average cost for tuition, room, and board at a private university is nearly $27,000 per year. Eighteen years from now, that cost is projected to almost triple, rising to approximately $79,000 per year. Now, you can begin to see how home stewardship is a financial vehicle and an investment tool that goes far beyond merely having a place to live. Clearly, this is an example of why buying is more profitable than renting. Overcoming the addiction of leasing can be beneficial in more ways than one.

Over time, purchasing a home has proven to be an effective wealth-building strategy for millions of Americans. *The median wealth of a low-income homeowner under age sixty-five is twelve times that of a similar renter.*

Most low-income households spend a third or more of their income on rent, none of which adds to their savings. Homeowners will begin to save immediately simply because part of their payment toward their housing now will pay down principal over time and accrue as home equity.

For an example, if a family purchases a home for $100,000 with a 5,000 down payment and the home price appreciates by 3 percent per year (very low), the home will be worth $115,927 after five years. And because the homeowners will have paid the loan down to approximately $90,000 over the same period, the equity will have grown by $20,853, for a 417 percent increase (33 percent annual return) on the initial $5,000 investment.

Purchasing a home is the largest investment that most families will ever make. Home stewardship has been called a "forced savings plan" in that the owner's payments on the mortgage principal are retained as **equity** as compared to other liquid assets. Wealth is accumulated to the extent that the value of the owner's equity exceeds any decline in the home's value.

Buying a home with a mortgage is a leveraged investment: even though only a small part of the purchase price is paid as a down payment (3.5 percent for FHA), the buyer controls all appreciation in the value of the property. However, the buyer absorbs any loss in value as well. Although of late property values have declined, general trend data on housing prices confirm that owner-occupied homes have performed well as long-term investments. However, many other factors can affect if and at what rate a home's value increases or decreases. For instance, changes in interest rates influence demand for housing and its attractiveness relative to other investments.

Home stewardship has become a critical factor in moving up the economic ladder. Sources indicate that home equity is the largest single source of household wealth for most Americans.

For minority homeowners in particular, home equity is an even more important component of wealth, representing more than three-fourths of their median net wealth. Similarly, for owners in the lowest income brackets, equity in single-family homes constitutes more than half their wealth.

Equity—the difference between what you owe on your mortgage loan and the value of the property—can help propel your net worth.

# Chapter 14

*It is one of the beautiful compensations of this life that no man can sincerely try to help another without helping himself.*
Ralph Waldo Emerson
American essayist and poet

### The Economic and Lifestyle Benefits of Home Stewardship

Although buying a home is a personal decision and includes a number of personal financial benefits, buying a home also helps our economy and our community. Your decision to purchase a home not only helps your personal economic system but it also helps the local economy in ways that you probably have not even thought of. Thus home stewardship is extremely important to keep our nation thriving. Because of your decision to purchase, you are helping companies stay in business, workers keep their jobs, and local schools retain funding. Streets are improved, local parks are established, and so on.

For years the real estate industry has been the pillar that has helped the economy stay vibrant. When you buy your home, you not only help yourself and your family, you also help the local and national economy.

Buying a home also changes your lifestyle. Take a moment and think about how living in an owner-occupied home compares to living in an apartment or in a family member's basement. Your life changes immediately through home stewardship. Even if it's simply an internal change, it's inevitable that your lifestyle will be uplifted. In addition, as you will read, this monumental decision also can have a very positive impact on your children's learning and development.

Throughout this century, there has been support for federal policies designed to encourage home ownership. Herbert Hoover called the owner-occupied home "a more wholesome, healthful, and happy atmosphere in which to raise children."

Lyndon Johnson promoted home ownership as part of a strategy for addressing the problems of the 1960s, declaring that "owning a home can increase responsibility and stake out a man's place in his community.... The man who owns a home has something to be proud of and reason to protect and preserve it."

Ronald Reagan said that home ownership "supplies stability and rooted nests."

Bill Clinton has linked increasing home ownership to the expansion of opportunity for working families. Speaking to the National Association of Realtors in November 1994, he expressed a national consensus that "more Americans should own their own homes, for reasons that are economic and tangible, and reasons that are emotional and intangible, but go to the heart of what it means to harbor, to nourish, to expand the American Dream."

Because the home-ownership rate fell from the 1980 to 1990, there was a huge push for the HUD secretary to work with leaders in the housing industry, representatives of nonprofit groups, and officials at all levels of government to develop a national home-ownership strategy that would increase home-ownership opportunities among populations and communities with lower-than-average ownership rates.

The National Homeownership Strategy cites four fundamental benefits:

*Through homeownership, a family...invests in an asset that can grow in value and...generate financial security.*

*Homeownership enables people to have greater control and exercise more responsibility over their living environment.*

*Homeownership helps stabilize neighborhoods and strengthen communities.*

*Homeownership helps generate jobs and stimulate economic growth.*

# Chapter 15

_One of the best and surest ways to stay broke is to pay more in taxes than you have to._
Derick W. Hungerford

## Tax Benefits of Home Stewardship

Homeowners also enjoy important tax advantages. The value and distribution of federal tax preferences for home stewardship, such as the deductibility of property taxes and mortgage interest and the one-time exclusion of capital gains, are great benefits for homeowners.

As tax-paying citizens, we are all responsible for meeting our obligation to the country. The deductions from our earned wages can sometimes seem like a burden. The smaller paycheck that results from tax deductions could ultimately lead to anxiety and cause us to feel oppressed by working every day and having nothing to show for it. Consider the fact that as a tenant, there are no breaks when it comes to taxes. In contrast, the United States of America so strongly supports the idea of you owning your own home that the government is willing to reward homeowners with tax relief.

Interest rates and real estate taxes are considered deductibles when filing your yearly income taxes with the IRS. Provisions in the Taxpayer Relief Act of 1997 allow homeowners to save between 20 to 40 cents in federal and state income taxes for every dollar spent on mortgage interest and property taxes.

## Tax Exclusion for the sale of your Home

For married couples, it is only necessary that one spouse hold the title to the home, but both must meet the two-year occupancy test to claim up to $500,000 in tax-free sales profit. There is no limit on how many times you can buy a house, live in it, and sell it for up to $250,000 in tax-free profits for each qualified seller. The only catch is that the seller must live in the house for two of the last five years as the primary residence.

There are even exemptions to the two-year occupancy test. If a homeowner must sell his or her house and it's been less than twenty four months of ownership and occupancy, a partial exemption is available if the sale is due to health reasons, changes of job location, or any other unforeseen circumstance as defined by the IRS. If the principle residency is sold in the year of a spouse's death, then the surviving spouse is still eligible to claim up to $500,000 in tax-free sales profit.

The rollover purchase income from the property sold can be used to trade-in or purchase another property without paying a tax. Additionally, deductions for qualifying expenses are available if you conduct a business from your home. All closing cost points that are paid are also tax deductible.

There are several tax deductions/write-offs that have major benefits for homeowners. We will discuss those specific benefits for people who are buying a home and people who currently own homes. To deduct the expenses of owning a home, you must file Form 1040 and itemize your deduction.

The major costs that are deductible as home-owner expenses are real estate taxes actually paid and interest paid on your mortgage loan. Some costs associated with buying a home may be deductible as well. Learning the tax rules can save you hundreds of thousands of dollars over the years. Wealthy families have figured this out. I often tell participants in my seminars that one of the best and surest ways to stay poor is to continue to pay more in taxes than you have to.

**The Tax Benefits of Owning:**

1.  A deduction for interest on your home mortgage (up to $1,000,000) or home-equity loan where available (up to $100,000).

2.  A deduction for losses that occur as a result of fire, storm, flood, earthquake, or other casualty, to the extent the loss exceeds $100 and 10 percent of your adjusted gross income (after reduction for insurance reimbursement).

3.  A deduction for purchase fees in the year they were paid. Keep a copy of your HUD1 settlement statement for your tax accountant.

4.  A deduction for qualifying expenses if you conduct a business in your home or rent out your residence and meet other requirements as defined in the law.

<u>Buying a Home</u>

Example

Purchase Price: $230,000.00 (4.5 percent rate)

Total interest paid in 1 year =   $10,350.00
Total taxes paid in 1 year =         $5,600.00
Total Tax Deduction =                  $15,950.00
(In the first year assuming that the borrower purchased the home in January 2012)

The government allows for a standard deduction for everyone (homeowners or renters).

If the buyer is a first-time home buyer, the tax advantage is the amount of total house deductions in excess of the standard deduction (standard deduction for a single return is $5950). In this case, by buying a home, the buyers have reduced the taxable income by $10,000.00; the difference between the standard deduction of $5950 and the total home deduction of $15,950.00. In this case, by buying a home, the buyers have reduced the taxable income by $12,200; the difference between the standard deduction of $5,800 and the total home deduction of $18,000.

If you paid $600 or more in mortgage interest during the year on any one mortgage, you should receive a Form 1098, *Mortgage Interest Statement*. The statement will show the total interest paid on your mortgage during the year. All interest is 100 percent tax deductible.

### Purchase Fees

Many times buyer may be required to pay origination fees called points, loan discount, maximum loan charges, or discount points. Points paid to get an original home mortgage may be fully deductible in the year paid.

You can only deduct points in the year paid if certain requirements are met:

- Your main home secures your loan (owner occupied primary residence).
- Paying points is normal and customary in the area where the loan was made.
- The amount is clearly shown on the settlement statement (HUD-1) as points charged for the mortgage. The point may be shown as paid from either your funds or the seller's.
- If you make less than $100,000 per year, FHA mortgage insurance is deductible.

### Property Taxes

Most state and local governments charge an annual tax on the value of real property. This is called a real estate tax. You can deduct the tax if it is based on the assessed value of the real property. In order to deduct these costs, you must have paid them either at settlement or to a taxing authority, either directly or through an escrow account.

You may deduct a division of real estate taxes. You and the seller each are considered to have paid your own share of the taxes, even if one or the other paid the entire amount. You each can deduct your own share if you itemize deductions for the year the property is sold. Real estate taxes are generally divided so that you and the seller each pay property taxes for the part of the tax year during which you owned the home. Your share of these taxes is fully deductible.

Many monthly house payments include an amount placed in escrow (put in the care of a third party) for real estate taxes. You may not be able to deduct the total you pay into the escrow account. You can only deduct the real estate taxes that the lender actually paid from escrow to the tax authority. In addition, you may be able to deduct special taxes for local benefits if the taxes are for maintenance, repair, or interest charges related to local benefits. Local benefits include the construction of streets, sidewalks, or water and sewer systems.

**Gain or Loss on the Sale**

Under the Tax Relief Act of 1997, you can obtain home-sale profits of up to $250,000 for a single person and $500,000 for a married couple and not pay a dime in income taxes.

If the amount realized on the sale is less than the adjusted basis, the difference is considered a loss. A loss on the sale of your main home cannot be deducted.

**Taxes and Expenses You Cannot Deduct**

Delinquent taxes are unpaid taxes that were imposed on the seller for an earlier tax year. If you agree to pay delinquent taxes when you bought your home, you cannot deduct them. You cannot deduct transfer taxes and similar taxes and charges on the sale of a personal home.

In addition you will not be able to deduct the following:

-Fire or homeowners insurance premiums
-FHA mortgage insurance premiums (if you make over 100,000)
-The amount applied to reduce the principal of the mortgage

## Home Buyer Tax Credit

In 2010, the government instituted a tax credit for home buyers. The credit was for a limited time only, it energized the housing market as thousands of new home buyers took advantage of the $8,000 tax credit for first-time home buyers.

A tax credit is kind of like a gift certificate that you can use to pay your taxes—it reduces your income tax bill on a dollar for dollar basis. Imagine paying your bill at IRS Restaurant, and then later getting an IRS Restaurant gift certificate. Normally, you would need to go back to IRS Restaurant and buy more food in order to use your new gift certificate. But what if IRS Restaurant allowed you to just turn in your gift certificate for cash? That's how the homebuyers tax credit worked. All you needed to do is file a form with the IRS after you bought your home, and the IRS would send you a refund check for $8,000 (or $6,500). Will the government implement the tax credit again, no one knows, however it will be a definite benefit if that is the case.

# Chapter 16

*Compound interest is the eighth natural wonder of the world and the most powerful thing I have ever encountered.*
Albert Einstein
Winner, Nobel Prize for Physics

## Investment Benefits of Home Stewardship

In the past, there has been great deal of discussion about the difference in lifetime earnings of a high school graduate versus a college graduate. The gap has closed somewhat, but it still remains. According to the US Department of Education National Center of Education, a high school graduate will earn an average of $31,900 per year over the span of his or her career, while a college graduate will earn an average of $51,000 per year. That's a difference of more than $1 million during their working careers. Thus, one may look at the cost of college as an investment, not just an expense.

Could there be a similar comparison between renting versus owning a house? How much wealth, on average, is created by buying a house? To understand this, we must better understand how owning a house creates wealth.

Increasingly, the house may be considered a key building block for wealth creation. Most people cite "buying a first house" as the reason they began saving for the first time.

When you buy a home, that act alone creates a more viable and secure financial future, but let's take it a step further. You have an opportunity to use your home to buy other investments, including rental properties, to generate a constant flow of income and build wealth. There are techniques you can use to create or fund your investment portfolio.

Let me start by making something very clear. You would never want to use your home to consume your equity. Over the years many homeowners have refinanced their homes to pay off credit cards and consumer debt. They then charged the credit cards up again and once again refinanced their home to pay off debt. They continued to do this to cover up their bad stewardship. This is called debt proliferation. Some homeowners bought time-shares, automobiles, and other things that decreased in value. Would you believe that some home owners actually used their equity to go on expensive vacations? They consumed all of their equity, and when the bubble burst, they could not use their homes to cover up their bad choices. This is the ultimate and surest way to lose your home very quickly. You should only use your home to add to your asset base. There are generally three strategies that will be appropriate when employing the investment benefits of your home:

1)   Funding home improvements—investing in your home
2)   Funding college expenses—investing in your child
3)   Funding investments/retirement—investing in your financial future

**Funding Home Improvements**

Many homeowners choose to complete various home improvement projects that will many times add to the value of their homes. One of the benefits of home stewardship that I mentioned earlier was being able to do what you want with your home. Whether it's upgrading your kitchen or bath or adding a hot tub on the deck off your bedroom, these improvements not only allow your home to reflect your personal style but can add to your equity appreciation and, in certain instances, increase your opportunities for tax deductions (check with your CPA to get specifics).

## Funding College Expenses

Many parents today feel it is their responsibility to pay for their children's education. For most this is a tremendous undertaking. The average cost of tuition at a four-year private university is $27,000. And this is not the total cost of attending college. In fact, tuition and fees constitute only 67 percent of the total budget for full-time students enrolled in a four-year private university and 36 percent of the budget for those attending four-year in-state, public institutions. The additional costs come from things such as transportation, books, supplies, and basic living expenses. Multiply those figures by the average 6.2 years students attending a four-year public college take to earn their degree, and the total adds up to more than $100,000!

One key to help with this large financial investment could be right under your nose—or more literally—over your head. Your home equity could ease the pending burden and improve your tax situation if properly structured.

## Funding Investment/Retirement

In the long run, the largest asset most people ever have at retirement is the equity in their own home. The average net worth of the typical American homeowner is $63,000. The average net worth of the typical renter is only $1,921.

Today it's hard saving for the future and many families are not able to save properly. A home is one way to open up doors of opportunity to create a comfortable financial future. Most people will not have enough money accumulated to finance a retirement that meets their needs, let alone their wants. However a home provides an opportunity you to use home equity to buy assets. In other words, you can "employ" your equity in certain instances to make money for you. I am certainly not speaking of risky investments, and for the vast majority of homeowners this will not be a strategy they should use. However, for those homeowners who intend to increase cash flow or increase investment portfolio, using their equity (if possible) will offer a viable solution to building a more comfortable financial future.

I personally have used this strategy to gain multiple investment properties that I now rent out. And yes, you must have the courage to get into the property investment world, but, for some, investing in real estate (if doing it the proper way) can pay dividends. This investment strategy is termed "pyramiding." This simply means using your initial property equity to gain or buy another home as an investment. This strategy can be repeated over and over again to acquire several homes that can potentially increase your cash flow. In order to do this, however, your mortgage payment will have to be lower than the rent you charge.

Another strategy is to use your equity to fund your investment or retirement accounts. The average Baby Boomer (those born between 1946 and 1964) has less than $50,000 saved for retirement. Unfortunately we won't be able to rely on Social Security. Taking ownership is the answer—through asset optimization and equity management with proper mortgage planning. Consult your tax accountant, financial planner, and mortgage planner for more details.

**A Word of Caution**

Between the years 2007–2010, the average homeowner lost 40% of their home's equity. Employing these strategies will depend on the market and the general affordability of these options. As I mentioned earlier, your home is like your business. When you "employ" your equity, you will have to pay what is essentially a monthly salary. Finding out if you can afford to hire your home is the key critical element to implementing any of these strategies. Again, for most homeowners, these strategies may not be viable or recommended. The purpose of including this section is for you to be aware of the various opportunities that come with buying a home. This information should not be used as recommendations because each homeowner is different. Please consult the proper professionals before attempting any of these financial strategies.

# Chapter 17

*Leverage is the one of the three financial miracles.*
Douglas Andrew
Author
Mortgage Programs and Funding

### VA Financing

This program is designed for eligible persons who served in the military on active duty or as a reservist. This program was established in 1944 and guaranteed a portion of the loan against foreclosure. The VA program allows for 100 percent financing and does not require a down payment. In addition, the seller can pay all closing costs on the buyer's behalf.

### FHA Mortgage

Federal Housing Administration loans were originally designed by the government to help low- and moderate- income families. FHA insures lenders against default by borrowers. Mortgage insurance is required no matter the size of the down payment. FHA loans are used in conjunction with most HUD approved down payment assistance programs. Currently, the required down payment for an FHA loan is 3.5 percent, and the seller can pay up to 6 percent of closing costs on the buyer's behalf.

### FHA 203K Full and Streamline

An FHA 203K loan can be used to acquire and "fix up" the property of your choice. This loan combines acquisition and improvement into one single loan, one payment, and one interest rate. The costs of improvements are funded in incremental payments as needed by the contractor. The 203K Full can be used for improvements costing $35,000 and more and will require an FHA 203K inspector to be involved. The 203K Streamline can be used for improvements priced below $35,000 and does not require the use of a 203K inspector. Both programs consist of a 3.5 percent down payment and will allow the seller to pay 6 percent of the buyer's closing costs.

### Buy Down

The buy down program is a variation of the fixed-rate mortgage. A buyer and seller can negotiate to pay the lender a sum of money at closing to reduce the buyer's monthly payment (interest rate) initially. The interest rate for the two-year period might be 6.5 percent, for example, and it is bought down to 4.5 percent the first year and 5.5 percent the second year. This enables the first-time homebuyer to qualify for a larger mortgage the first year. The second year is still affordable with an addition of only 1 percent interest, with the third year reaching the rate 6.5 percent, which will remain the fixed rate for the term of the loan.

### Adjustable-Rate Mortgage

The adjustable-rate mortgage (ARM) was developed in the late 1970s and quickly became popular because of the low initial payment. The ARM payment will vary throughout the term of the loan and involves monthly payments that are subject to changes in the interest rate as a result of a predetermined index (one, three, or five years as an example).

This loan has three characteristics: an **initial interest rate**—the interest rate offered at the beginning of the ARM loan, an **interest rate cap**—a limit placed on how much the interest rate can increase or decrease during any adjustment period, and a **conversion clause**—a clause that allows the borrower to change the ARM to a fixed rate loan at some point during the term of the mortgage.

### Conventional Fixed Rate

The conventional fixed rate is the standard product used by most lending institutions. Years ago conventional loans required 20 percent down. Now conventional loans are more flexible and do not require a large down payment. Typical down payments range from 5–10 percent, and there is no fluctuation in the interest rate throughout the term of the loan.

### Forty-Year Fixed-Rate Mortgage

Similar to the conventional thirty-year mortgage, the forty-year mortgage will allow you to stretch your payment to forty years. Payments will be lower due to the ten additional years. Payments are consistent, and the program requires a down payment of 3–10 percent. The seller will be allowed to pay up to 3 percent of closing costs.

### Interest-Only Loan

This program allows you to make payments toward only the interest on your loan. The principle is not decreased during the term of the loan. Payments are usually lower than they would be if they included principle. This program can be offered in conjunction with a thirty-year term or a twenty-year term (after ten years the note would change to a principle and interest payment).

### Construction-to-Permanent Mortgages

The construction-to-permanent mortgage combines construction loan parameters with long-term permanent financing. A construction loan usually runs from four to twelve months and is designed to finance the construction of a new home (new home complex or builder site). It differs from a permanent loan, which normally runs from fifteen to thirty years. With a construction-to-permanent loan there is only one closing, but two objectives are met: (1) a loan is obtained to cover the building of the structure, and (2) the long-term financing is secured. When the construction phase has ended, the loan converts to permanent financing. A construction-to-permanent loan is most often granted when land is owned outright.

### Bridge Loans

Bridge loans span the gap between the end of one loan and the start of a brand-new loan. The most common use of a bridge loan is to obtain the equity from a current residence to use for the down payment or closing costs of a new home. After the new home has been settled, the bridge loan would be satisfied through the sale of the old property. Bridge loans are typically for six-month terms with a renewal option for another six months.

### Reverse Annuity Mortgages

The interest rate on reverse annuity mortgages (RAMs) is usually fixed, and the payments are not included. This loan is due when the home is sold or upon the death of the borrower. The term may be fixed and have refinancing options.

A reverse annuity mortgage is attractive to borrowers on fixed incomes who need the equity to supplement their monthly incomes while continuing to own, live in, and maintain the property. With this mortgage, the lender appraises the home and offers a loan based upon a certain percentage of the home's current value. The payments are made directly to the borrower by the lender. The loan repayment is due on a specific date, upon the sale of the property, or upon the death of the borrower, whichever comes first.

### Land Installment Contracts

A land installment contract is a quasi loan: the borrower makes payments without possessing the title or ownership. The title is not conveyed until a certain number of payments are made or the property has been refinanced. The borrower has equity interest only. If one payment is missed, the borrower could lose the property. This agreement was popular when interest rates were high and homes were sold with loans that could not be assumed.

### Energy Efficient Mortgage

The energy efficient mortgage (EEM) has been around since the late 1970s. With an EEM, the borrower can increase the mortgage loan by as much as an additional $8,000.00 to install energy conservation measures such as storm windows, solar panels, and automatic thermostats. The loan payments rise accordingly, but the borrower's savings on the utility bills over the life of the loan normally equal or surpass the installment costs. The improvements can also raise the resale value of the home and, in some cases, can raise property values.

### USDA Loan

The United States Department of Agriculture (USDA) loan allows buyers to purchase a home with no money down. This 100 percent financing program is geared toward purchases of homes in certain rural areas. Unlike most other loans, this program does not require mortgage insurance. There is a funding fee, similar to VA and FHA that will be financed within the loan. This program also allows the seller to pay up to 6 percent of the buyer's closing costs.

### $100-Down FHA

The $100-down FHA is a great program for those with vision and a willingness to make improvements to a home. This program allows you to purchase a designated home for $100 down. Visit HUD's website to view homes that are available. Most likely, you will be using the 203K loan to complete needed improvements. This program allows for the seller to pay up to 6 percent of the buyer's closing costs.

## Officers and Teachers Next Door Program

The Officers and Teachers Next Door Program is an FHA loan that was designed for those serving our community. Law enforcement officers, pre-Kindergarten through twelfth grade teachers, firefighters, and emergency medical technicians can contribute to community revitalization while becoming homeowners through HUD's Good Neighbor Next Door Sales Program. HUD offers a substantial incentive in the form of a discount of 50 percent from the list price of the home. In return you must commit to live in the property for thirty-six months as your sole residence. This program allows for the seller to pay up to 6 percent of the buyer's closing costs.

## Home Path Program

The Home Path program is for specifically designated properties owned by Fannie Mae. The down payment for this program is 3 percent. No PMI is required and many times an appraisal isn't required. This program allows you to complete home improvement tasks similar to the 203K financing program. Sellers are allowed to contribute up to 6 percent of the buyer's closing costs.

## Funding (DPA) Opportunities

### Neighborhood Stabilization Program

The Neighborhood Stabilization Program (NSP) was established for the purpose of stabilizing communities that have suffered from foreclosures and abandonment. Through the purchase and redevelopment of foreclosed and abandoned residential properties this program is intended to strengthen our community. The program parameters vary but give a certain amount of money toward the buyer's down payment and/or closing costs. This grant has specific occupancy term requirements and approval qualifications.

### American Dream Down Payment Initiative

The American Dream Down payment Initiative (ADDI) provides down payment and closing cost assistance to low- to moderate-income families who are first-time homebuyers for the purchase of single family housing that will serve as the buyers primarily home. There are income restrictions for this program, and occupancy requirements apply. This program can be used in conjunction with the FHA program.

### Home Purchase Assistance Program

The Home Purchase Assistance Program (HPAP) enables lower- and moderate-income individuals and families to purchase affordable housing in Washington, D.C. Qualified HPAP applicants can receive up to $44,000 in financial assistance to purchase single-family houses, condominiums, and cooperative apartments. HPAP funds can be used for down payment and/or closing costs. The HPAP assistance comes in the form of a low interest five-year deferred loan. Loan amounts are determined by a combination of factors, including income, household size, and the assets that an applicant can commit toward the purchase of a home. In addition, all loan recipients are required to maintain their properties in compliance with D.C. housing codes.

## My Home

The My Home loan provides home loan assistance to eligible first-time homebuyers to purchase owner occupied or vacant residential properties anywhere in Prince Georges County. Home purchase assistance includes down payment and/or mortgage principle reduction costs and/or closing costs. Occupancy term requirements apply, along with approval qualifications. Home buyers can receive up to 5 percent of the purchase price for down payment and/or closing costs.

## Community Development Administration

The Community Development Administration (CDA) program is a statewide DPA program for first-time homebuyers and assists with the down payment and closing costs. Income restrictions are more flexible as compared to other grant programs. Funds from this program can be used for down payment and/or closing costs.

## HOC Program

The Housing Opportunity Commission program is designed to assist HOC residents in becoming financially prepared to purchase a home in Montgomery County. (A HOC resident is someone who participates in a HOC program and/or lives in a property owned or managed by HOC). This program offers down payment and closing cost assistance to qualified home buyers.

## College Park Program

The City of College Park offers $5000 in grant assistance, on a first-come, first-served basis, to encourage the conversion of single-family rental properties to owner-occupied housing and to encourage police officers and city employees to make their homes in College Park. Funds are provided at settlement for use toward purchase of the property and participants may use grant funds in conjunction with other housing programs.

Anyone purchasing a single-family property that was previously rented for a minimum of two years is eligible for a $5,000 grant.

A full-time certified police officer employed by the Maryland State Police, Prince George's County Police, Maryland-National Capital Park & Planning Police, Metro Transit Police or the University of Maryland Police is eligible for a $5,000 grant toward the purchase of any city property including condominium apartments.

A full-time employee of the City of College Park is eligible for a $5,000 grant toward the purchase of any city property including condominium apartments.

### MAP Program

The Mortgage Assistance Program (MAP) is designed for first time homebuyers needing assistance with down payments, closing costs, and reducing first mortgage amounts. Depending on your need, this program can provide up to $30,000 in assistance. The funds are provided as a loan; however, no payments are required and the funds are loaned at zero percent interest. MAP loan amounts must be repaid when you sell your home, transfer the title, or in 30 years, whichever occurs first. Under certain circumstances you may be required to repay the MAP loan if you refinance your first mortgage. This program is intended for home buyers purchasing in Anne Arundel County.

### Buy Suitland Program

The Buy Suitland Program was designed for first time homebuyers interested in purchasing a home in Suitland, Maryland. Suitland is the home to the Suitland Federal Center employing over 12,000 and a Metro station, is slated for a 22-acre mixed-use development project, and now has its own First-Time Homebuyer Program. The Buy Suitland Initiative will award 0% interest grants to households who have not owned a home within the last 3 years, and are buying a home as their principal residence

## Baltimore Program

Baltimore City offers a variety of incentive programs to home-buyers. Each program has specific qualifications, managed by different city departments or nonprofits. These programs range from $4000—$40,000 in down payment and closing cost assistance.

# Chapter 18

---

*When two or more people coordinate in a spirit of harmony and work toward a definite objective or purpose, they place themselves in position, through the alliance, to absorb power directly from the great storehouse of Infinite Intelligence.*
Napoleon Hill
Author, *Think and Grow Rich*

## How to Find a Good Mortgage Consultant

Buying a home may be one your biggest undertakings, so it's vital that you find a professional that has your best interests at heart and who is knowledgeable. Between the years of 2004 and 2006, tons of people entered in the business of mortgages with no experience, no commitment, no character, and bad conduct. As a matter of fact 65 percent of all loan officers in the business in 2006 had only been in the business for three years.

Always make sure you are working with an experienced, professional lender. The largest financial transaction of your life is far too important to place into the hands of someone who is not capable of advising you properly and troubleshooting the issues that may arise along the way.

The number one question that new homebuyers ask is "What is your interest rate? While this is a valid question, it certainly isn't the most important one. Remember, this is the biggest investment that you will probably ever make; I advise against making this monumental decision on just one piece of the puzzle. Interest rates change daily and sometimes several times during the day. Furthermore, a low interest rate on the wrong program will land you into foreclosure. The key to having a successful mortgage is working with a character-driven mortgage professional. Doing this will guarantee that you receive a competitive rate along with the right program for you.

Curious prospective home buyers sometimes turn to Internet-based services just to see what current interest rates are. But a faceless web site will not take your future financial planning into consideration or guide you through the many nuances of the loan process.

When shopping for a home loan, be wary of web-based services that offer programs to reel prospects in with attractive rates that are based upon unrealistic time frames.

If a lender is offering a terrific rate based on a 10-day lock-in period, it is unlikely that the potential home owner would actually be able to find their dream home, get through the negotiation process and win approval from a lender within such a short period of time. This is called *short-pricing*, and when it comes time to close the transaction, the rate that was originally offered is simply no longer available. As a result, the unfortunate prospect is bulldozed into a loan program with a higher interest rate.

It is highly unlikely that a qualified loan originator whose business is based upon referrals will use unscrupulous tactics such as this to get new customers in the door!

I am a part of a Mortgage Community and Educational Organization called Mortgage Market Guide Inc. According to our training, the following are several questions that can help you to make a good choice. The lender absolutely must be able to answer correctly. If the answers are not acceptable or the lender does not know the answers, leave immediately and go to a lender that does.

**Market Questions:**

**1)  What are mortgage interest rates based on?**

The only correct answer is Mortgage Baked Securities or Mortgage Bonds, not the Fed or the 10-year Treasury Note. While the 10-year Treasury Note sometimes trends in the same direction as Mortgage bonds, it is not unusual to see them move in completely opposite directions. Do not work with a lender who has their eyes on the wrong indicators.

**2)   What is the next Economic Report or event that could cause interest rate movement?**

A professional lender will have this at their fingertips and should have an up to date weekly calendar of weekly economic reports and events that may cause rates to fluctuate.

**3)   When Bernanke and the Fed "change rates", what does this mean…and what impact does this have on mortgage interest rates?**

The answer may surprise you. When the Fed makes a move, they are changing a rate called the "Fed Funds Rate". This is a very short-term rate that impacts credit cards, credit lines, auto loans and the like. Mortgage rates most often will actually move in the opposite direction as the Fed change, due to the dynamics within the financial markets.

**4)   What is happening in the market today and what do you see in the near future?**

If a lender cannot explain how Mortgage Bonds and interest rates are moving at the present time, as well as what is coming up in the near future, you are talking with someone who is still reading last week's newspaper, and probably not a professional with whom to entrust your home mortgage financing.

More than likely, this is one of the largest and most important financial transactions you will ever make. You might do this only four or five times in your entire life, but a professional does this every single day. Make sure to work with someone who is experienced and has your best interest at heart.

**Background and Experience Questions:**

1)  **How long have you been working as a mortgage loan officer?**

I am sure there are good loan officers that have limited experience. However, do you really want a loan officer working on your transaction who has been in the business for only one or two years? As I've indicated, this transaction will probably be the biggest financial obligation you have. Making sure you are working with someone who has the experience necessary will be very important to having a successful transaction.

2)  **How many transactions have you been involved with? Do you have any reference letters?**

First of all, if the loan officer answers this question by indicating the number of "loans" he closed, you know that you are dealing with someone who is number based and not relationship based. This question should be answered in terms of families served, not loans closed. In addition, if the loan officer has only helped five or ten families, you will want to reevaluate the experience level of the professional you are dealing with. If the loan officer cannot show you letters from satisfied clients then maybe none of the clients were satisfied. Do your due diligence.

3)  **What is your lending philosophy?**

If they don't have a philosophy that is a problem right there. A lending philosophy should center around helping clients with the best possible rates, with competitive costs, and a solid program. A good lending philosophy puts your interest ahead of the company's interest.

A good lending philosophy is driven by character and excellent conduct.

**4)    Do you own a home yourself? Describe your experience.**

I often get a chuckle when I mention this question in my seminars. But isn't this important? You would be surprised at the number of Loan Officers who were/are participating in the mortgage industry who did not even own a home themselves. How would this Loan Officer ever be able to help you to get through this experience if they have not experienced home stewardship themselves? It's impossible for them to share the benefits and blessing of Home stewardship if they haven't experienced it themselves.

Once you are satisfied that you are working with a top-quality professional mortgage advisor, here are the rules and secrets you must know to "shop" effectively.

**First, IF IT SEEMS TOO GOOD TO BE TRUE, IT PROBABLY IS.** But you didn't really need me to tell you that did you? Mortgage money and interest rates all come from the same places, and if something sounds really unbelievable, better ask a few more questions and find the hook. Is there a prepayment penalty? If the rate seems incredible, are there extra fees? What is the length of the lock-in? If fees are discounted, is it built into a higher interest rate?

**Second, YOU GET WHAT YOU PAY FOR.** If you are looking for the cheapest deal out there, understand that you are placing a hugely important process into the hands of the lowest bidder. Best case; expect very little advice, experience and personal service. Worst case; expect that you may not close at all. All too often, you don't know until it's too late that cheapest isn't necessarily the BEST. However, if you want the cheapest quote—head on out to the Internet, and I wish you the best. Just remember that if you've heard any horror stories from family members, friends or coworkers about missed closing dates, or big surprise changes at the last minute on interest rate or costs...these are often due to working with discount or internet lenders who may have a serious lack of experience. Most importantly, remember that the cheapest rate on the wrong strategy can cost you thousands more in the long run.

Third, **MAKE CORRECT COMPARISONS.** When looking at estimates, don't simply look at the bottom line. You absolutely must compare lender fees to lender fees, as these are the only ones that the lender controls. And make sure lender fees are not "hidden" down amongst the title or state fees. A lender is responsible for quoting other fees involved with a mortgage loan, but since they are third-party fees—they are often under-quoted up front by a lender to make their bottom line appear lower, since they know that many consumers are not educated to NOT simply look at the bottom line! APR? Easily manipulated as well, and worthless as a tool of comparison.

Fourth, **UNDERSTAND THAT INTEREST RATES AND CLOS-ING COSTS GO HAND IN HAND.** This means that you can have any interest rate that you want—but you may pay more in costs if the rate is lower than the norm. On the other hand, you can pay discounted fees, reduced fees, or even no fees at all—but understand that this comes at the expense of a higher interest rate. Either of these balances might be right for you, or perhaps somewhere in between. It all depends on what your financial goals are. A professional lender will be able to offer the best advice and options in terms of the balance between interest rate and closing costs that correctly fits your personal goals.

Fifth, **UNDERSTAND THAT INTEREST RATES CAN CHANGE DAILY, EVEN HOURLY.** This means that if you are comparing lender rates and fees—this is a moving target on an hourly basis. For example, if you have two lenders that you just can't decide between and want a quote from each—you must get this quote at the exact same time on the exact same day with the exact same terms or it will not be an accurate comparison. You also must know the length of the lock you are looking for, since longer rate locks typically have slightly higher rates.

Again, my advice to you is to be smart. Ask questions. Get answers.

# Chapter 19

---

*A journey of 1000 miles must begin with one step.*
Ancient Chinese Proverb
**Buying Real Estate**

Just as finding the right mortgage professional is important, so is making sure you are working with a professional and character-driven realtor. Your agent is the link to you and the property you ultimately choose. Your agent will be presenting a contract to the seller on your behalf, and it will be very important that the agent has your best interests at heart. If you received this book from your agent, more than likely he or she cares about your well-being and wants to help you along your journey.

### The Importance of Using a Real Estate Agent

Using an experienced real estate agent can help you navigate through the searching process with ease.

An agent who is a member of the Multiple Listing Service can help you identify more homes for sale as opposed to you looking yourself.

An agent can help you can provide important data that will help you choose a home effectively.

As you can see, an experienced agent can be tremendous help in your search for a house.

It's important to note, the agent in a real estate transaction is legally the agent of the seller, and is legally obligated to act in the seller's best interest.

Agent Chuck helps the seller decide on an asking price, advertises the house, includes it in the Multiple Listing Service, and shows the house to qualified potential purchasers. If Agent Chuck, the listing agent, sells the house to one of his clients, he is entitled to the full commission, which is paid by the seller from the proceeds of the sale.

Another realtor Agent Angela "researches the MLS and thinks that it could be the house her clients are hoping for. Agent Angela shows the house to the Browns, and they decide to make an offer to purchase the house. The offer is accepted and the sales contract is signed. In this case, Agent Angela, known as the selling agent, and Agent Chuck, the listing agent, will share the commission.

**The important point to remember is that both agents represent the seller.** Even though agent Angela worked with the buyer and spent a great deal of time showing them homes, etc., she is paid by and work for the seller.

### Agent Chuck's responsibility to the seller

- Advertise the property and handle calls about the ad.
- Qualify prospective clients and make arrangements to show the house to those who qualified.
- Deliver offers to purchase to the seller.
- Relay the seller's response back to the potential buyer when a decision is made.
- Represent the property at its listed price and terms as set by the seller and avoid revealing privileged information concerning the seller's situation
- Complete the transaction after a contract has been signed by both parties.

- Arrange to meet with inspectors and appraisers, and provide necessary paperwork for others involved in the process.
- Attend the closing.

**Agent Angela's responsibility**

An agent offers his or her time, experience, and expertise to the buyer with the expectation of obtaining a fee when the house is sold. Such agents do have certain obligations to buyers:

- Use reasonable care and skill in performing their duties.
- Deal with clients honestly and fairly.
- Disclose all facts known to the agent that affect the value or desirability of the property that are not known to the buyer.

In dealing with a buyer, an agent who represents the seller must comply with applicable real estate laws. For example, while it is not illegal to exaggerate the desirability of a house, it is considered fraud if the agent intentionally misrepresents the property or steers the buyer to or from any specific neighborhood.

**Using a Buyer's Broker**

The biggest advantage is that the buyer's broker works for you, not the seller. Buyer's brokers may not show as much bias in which house you buy and may be quicker to point out problems in a house.

**Choosing a Real Estate Agent**

When you are looking for an agent, consider the following:

Credentials—State laws require real estate brokers and sales professionals to be licensed in order to protect the public from fraud, dishonesty, or incompetence in real estate transactions. In every state, applicants for a real estate license must meet certain educational requirements and pass an examination to show that they have an adequate knowledge of the business. They must also renew their license every two years and must follow certain standards of conduct as established by the state Real Estate Commission.

- **A *real estate broker*** is a person licensed to carry out real estate transactions and to receive a fee for these activities.
- **A *real estate salesperson*** is also licensed, but he or she must operate under the supervision of a licensed broker because the training is not as advanced as that of a broker.
- **A *realtor*** is a licensed real estate agent who is a member of the Association of Realtors. The Association, which has local, state, and national chapters, is a trade association, which promotes high standards in the real estate profession.

Experience—There's no substitute for experience. Word of mouth referrals are among the best ways to locate an experienced broker. Ask friends, relatives, and coworkers to recommend someone they've worked with.

Service Area—The agent you choose should be well-established in the areas where you are interested in buying and have working knowledge of the area, the services available, current market conditions, schools, and so forth.

Professionalism—Agents should also follow up on their commitments, keep you informed of what's going on, and conduct themselves in a businesslike manner.

### Using More Than One Agent

In most instances, you'll need only one agent. Working with several agents creates confusion and wasted effort all around, particularly if all the agents you select are members of MLS. Although competition between agents may lead them to work harder to find the perfect house for you, it generally leads to an unnecessary duplication of effort. One exception to this may be when you are considering homes in two different communities located a large distance apart. In this case, it may make sense to have an agent in each of these areas. This way, you'll have the benefit of each agent's knowledge of his or her service area. However, most of the time having one agent will suit you just fine.

As I've mentioned earlier, the home buying process can be a daunting task. It will be very important that you have calm and level headed professionals in your corner including the Mortgage Loan Officer and the Realtor. The job for these professionals is to "protect" you from inescapable twist, turns, bumps and hiccups of the process. I've worked with Realtors who were AWESOME in managing their client's expectations and offering calm and assuring words of encouragement throughout the process. On the other hand, I've worked with other Real Estate Agents who did the very opposite. I am hoping that you will select an agent that is professional, knowledgeable and able to keep you grounded, focused and positioned to finish the process strong.

(see workbook for specific questions to ask)

**For Sale by Owner Properties**

The main advantage to for sale by owner properties (FSBOs) is that the agent's commission will not be added into the sale price, making these homes somewhat less expensive. Take extra precautions to have the home inspected before you buy, and have an attorney advise you on drawing up the sales contract.

# Chapter 20

---

*You must take personal responsibility. You cannot change the circum-
stances, the seasons, or the wind, but you can change yourself.*
Jim Rohn, business philosopher

### The Ten Greatest Mistakes a Person Can Make When Financing a Home

Our economy has suffered tremendously over the last few years, primarily due to the downslide of the mortgage and financial markets. I believe that now more than ever, it's important to make decisions about your mortgage to include your overall short- and long-term financial goals. I believe that many of the victims of the recent foreclosure epidemic would have escaped these financially difficult times by avoiding the mistakes and pitfalls of financing a home. A mortgage may be both the biggest asset and debt you'll have in life. Therefore it's extremely important to have clarity when applying for one. Over the last few years, mortgage loans have become a commodity of sorts, which hasn't worked out for many homeowners. Instead, finding the right mortgage *for you* is all about relationship. Having a professional, experienced, character-driven mortgage consultant will pay you dividends for years to come. Because I've heard so many stories about mortgage tragedies over the last seventeen years of my career, I thought it was imperative to provide some warnings to help you navigate through today's mortgage market.

### Mistake 1: We Don't Have a Relationship with a Certified Mortgage Planning Specialist

A person will form several business relationships over a lifetime. These include relationships with a doctor, attorney, accountant, financial planner, and even barber or beautician—yet you don't find that many people have a consistent relationship with a mortgage banker.

In the past, homeowners averaged a new home loan only once every seven years. But because interest rates have been so low, the average has gone up due to the number of times homeowners are refinancing to get lower rates. Despite this, many homeowners/home-buyers do not have a relationship with a mortgage lender because the need for the home financing still arises much less often than the need to get a haircut.

This lack of mortgage-related relationships is not only the consumers' fault. With the mortgage industry going through major ups and downs and the changing economic cycles, sometimes mortgage companies come and go. Regardless of the reason, if you have no relationship with a qualified mortgage professional, you are less likely to find qualified advice when you need it. When rates go down, you could be one of thousands trying to get refinancing options; you will have little time to develop a relationship with a qualified professional that you know has your best interests at heart. Once you find a reliable Mortgage Consultant, I would suggest you add him/her to your team of experts and hold them responsible for checking in with you yearly for an Annual Mortgage Review (AMR). This way you will be well aware of the market changes and opportunities.

### Mistake 2: We Have No Idea Whether the Lender We Pick Is Qualified

Because we do not have a long-term relationship with a certified mortgage planning specialist, we do not tend to shop for a mortgage correctly. We know how to ask about a mortgage company's rates (or, at least we think we do) but not the background of the company or the individual with whom we are dealing. For example, what is the experience level of the loan officer? Most major mortgage companies do not have formal training programs, due to industry transition. Require a resume from the person with whom you are working. It would make sense to get an idea of the company's background and the company's business philosophy as well. Community involvement is important as well. As lenders, we ask you "a million" questions...why not interview your loan officer as well?

**Mistake 3: We Do Not Know How to Shop for a Mortgage.**

As mentioned previously, the most popular question during mortgage shopping is, "What is the current mortgage interest rate?" Most homebuyers/homeowners don't know that there are a variety of programs available and that future plans will have a major impact on the type of program, including whether or not to get a loan that will require you to pay mortgage insurance. Although asking for the current interest rate is a *very important* question, it may not be the best question. Low rates can be quoted at any point and changed at the last minute by mortgage loan officers who do not have your best interests at heart. That is why it is paramount to be comfortable with whom you choose as your mortgage loan officer more so than with the interest rate quoted. A person with principles will not change the rate at the last minute. A person with principles will make sure that all information shared is honest and accurate. As a consumer, it's advisable to find a competitive rate, on the right program, from a trusted advisor. Shopping doesn't simply mean looking for the best rate.

**Mistake 4: We Do Not Stay Consistent with the Initial Plan of Action.**

Lack of consistency with the original plan can be caused by a variety of uncontrollable factors, such as loss of job, car repairs, family emergency, and so on. However, there are cases when the urge to get that new TV or, better yet, buy that new Mercedes causes a conflict with the original goal. By the way, that actually happened in my experience. Several years ago, a client actually purchased a Mercedes Benz two weeks before closing. Needless to say, she was not able to get her new home at that time. Remember the sacrifice: you will be required to make one. Some home seekers unfortunately can't seem to suppress their desire for immediate gratification in order to get something even better. It's important to stay focused on your biggest goal while going through the process.

**Mistake 5: We Think We Know What Type of Mortgage We Would Like Without Knowing the Major Mortgage Options**.

Many begin by shopping for a thirty-year fixed mortgage (which in my opinion is the safest type of mortgage for a first-time homebuyer) or a one-year adjustable. With only one or two options, we often make our decisions based only on what we are familiar with. There are several additional major mortgage types that should be considered. The best option for you may change with your own changing financial plans or changes in the economic environment.

For example, If you are going to be in a home for a long period of time, you may want to stretch your loan out to a thirty- or even forty-year term. Allow your equity to grow as you continue to pay off your mortgage, and allow inflation to work for you while paying your loan back with cheaper dollars.

If you are nearing retirement *and* plan to stay in your home, you may want to consider a short-term fixed rate because your income at that point will be fixed. If your current income can support paying a higher note, then a fifteen-year term may be advisable so that your home will be paid soon after retirement.

If you plan to move within three years, you may want to look into a one-, three- or five-year adjustable. This way you get the lowest rate possible, which will allow you to save for your next purchase.

The point here is that you may not want to shop for a particular type of mortgage but shop for your particular need. You should work with a professional to evaluate which is best for you under your present financial scenario.

### A Note for you after you buy your home

Many homeowners who decide to refinance their home loan forget about the long term. Refinancing without a plan is dangerous. Always think about the end result before pursuing. You must stay in the house long enough to recoup the closing costs. There are specific reasons to refinance that can help you in the financial long-run; however, there are reasons that are not good for refinancing as well. Your home should **not** be used to consume your equity. Your home should only be used to increase your asset base.

The type of mortgage you select will dramatically affect your net worth and directly impact your ability to retire. A proper strategy takes in consideration the time you'll be living in the home, income projections, and retirement needs and all play a very critical role in determining which mortgage is right for you

### Mistake 6: We Do Not Understand the Terms of the Loan Applied For

Making sure you understand the terms of your particular loan Is critical in being a successful home steward. One of the most important documents in your settlement paperwork is your *note*. The note describes your loan type, your interest rate, the term, if you had a prepayment penalty, and when you would expect to pay off your loan. Reading this one document could have helped many of the homeowners who are unfortunately suffering through an undesirable mortgage loan. The note will be presented at closing; however, there are other documents that confirm these very same items. Make sure to read your Good Faith Estimate, Truth in Lending, and all disclosures that you are required to sign.

## Mistake 7: We Listen to Too Many People outside the Transaction

In the multitude of counselors there is safety. However, talking to too many people.can be detrimental. Everyone's situation is different and can't be compared to yours. Furthermore, too many people's opinion can cloud your judgment and cause confusion. One of the five keys of having a successful home-buying experience is to protect your confidence. The right mortgage loan officer will give you enough information to empower you without confusing you. Try not to talk with numerous nonprofessional homeowners who may not know all the detailed information concerning your profile.

## Mistake 8: We Get Tied into Looking at Homes before Getting a Solid Preapproval.

One of the biggest mistakes you can make is looking for a home prior to getting a solid loan preapproval. That is like waking up in the morning and jumping into your car to go on a two-week vacation without planning your trip. You may eventually arrive at a destination; however, there will be obstacles, such as running out of gas, getting lost, or not finding lodging. Would you like a vacation experience like that? It's important to have proper planning and know where you are and what is required to get to your destination. Getting your approval is vitally important and will give you the peace of mind in knowing that your financing has been secured. Many home seekers have started the home search process, only to find later that they do not qualify for a mortgage loan. Another improper strategy is being easily persuaded into looking at homes that cost more than you can afford. To take it a step further, if you are in the process of cleaning your credit with hopes of purchasing a home soon, you still should wait until you get your preapproval before searching. If a realtor continues to send you listings, knowing that you are not quite ready to purchase, I strongly suggest that you find out their motivation. Think about this carefully: why would a real estate agent send you homes to view if you are not ready to purchase? Searching for a home prior to your approval puts your focus on the home and not on what you need to do in order to buy that home, which is where the focus should be. Looking for a home may be the more pleasant part of the journey; however, searching before your loan preapproval impedes your progress by putting extra pressure and emotion in the process.

**Mistake 9: We allow the Loan Officer to tell us what to pay on a monthly basis**

One of the first questions I usually like to ask first time buyers is "what is your desired payment". I believe that is a very good question because it allows you to set your own budget. As lenders, we base your payments on your gross income. As a consumer, you will make your payment from your net income. Just because a Loan Officer tells you that you "qualify" for a $2000 payment as an example, does not necessarily mean that you can actually afford a $2000 payment. Make sure you set your own budget.

**Mistake 10: We Allow the Process to Become Emotional**

Buying a home is a good choice. However, trading your peace for the home is not advisable. Many home searchers find themselves caught in the trap of emotionalism as they pursue their dream of home stewardship. This can cause unnecessary frustration and can lead to a settlement but also a lack of fulfillment. Making decisions while being emotionally tied to a situation can lead to bad choices. Make this decision a logical one. Yes, it's an important decision, and it will more than likely give you enjoyment after you've closed escrow and begin making your house your home. However, a home doesn't make you, and it should not determine your value. If this is your season to purchase, that is an awesome thing. If not, try again later". As the psalmist sings, "What God has for you, it is for you." Nothing can stand in the way. If you do your part, have patience, and keep your character, your dream will become a reality.

# Chapter 21
# Twenty Terms You Should Know

1. **Adjustable-Rate Mortgage (ARM)**—Also referred to as a variable-rate mortgage—a mortgage in which the interest rate is adjusted periodically based on a preselected index.

2. **Annual Percentage Rate (APR)**—An interest rate that reflects the cost of a mortgage as a yearly rate. This rate takes into account any points and fees (closing costs) and is based on the loan going to its full term. APR can often be manipulated by lenders and is often inaccurate with adjustable-rate mortgages.

3. **Appraisal**—A written report containing an estimate of property value and the data on which the estimate is based. Appraisals are prepared by a licensed appraiser who is independent of the seller, buyer, lender, and real estate agent.
    The appraiser inspects the subject property and compares it with other similar properties that have sold in the area to determine the fair market value.
    The mortgage lender bases the loan-to-value ratio on the lesser of the purchase price or appraised value on a purchase transaction. If you are refinancing a property, an issue called "seasoning" may come into play. This affects which value the lender allows you to use when determining the mortgage balance.

4. **Assumption**—An agreement between buyer and seller in which the buyer assumes responsibility for the seller's existing mortgage. This agreement could potentially save the buyer money because closing costs and the current interest rates, possibly higher, do not ap-

ply. In most residential mortgage transactions, this is not an option because the seller's existing mortgage normally has a "due on sale" clause that requires the seller to pay off the mortgage if the house is sold or if the ownership is transferred.

5. **Buy-Down**—A method of lowering the buyer's monthly payment for a short period of time. The lender or homebuilder subsidizes the mortgage by lowering the interest rate for the first few years of a loan. This strategy can be very effective in today's market.

6. **Closing**—Also referred to as "settlement." The meeting at the conclusion of a real estate sale in which the property and funds are exchanged between the parties involved.

7. **Closing Costs**—The total points and fees that are associated with completing a mortgage transaction or a house purchase or sale. Often a good negotiation strategy for both the buyer and seller is for the seller to pay closing costs on behalf of the buyer.

8. **Deb-to-Income Ratio**—The ratio, expressed as a percentage, that results from dividing a borrower's monthly payment obligation on long-term debts by the borrower's gross monthly income.

9. **Down Payment**—Cash paid by the buyer at closing that makes up the difference between purchase price and the mortgage amount.

10. **Earnest Money**—Money given by a buyer to a seller as a deposit to commit the buyer to the future transaction. Earnest money is subtracted from closing costs.

11. **Equity**—The value an owner has in real estate over and above the obligation against the property. Equity is fair market value minus the current mortgage and other liens. Real estate equity should be managed just like any other investment.

12. **Escrow**—Funds given to a third party that will be held to cover payments such as tax or insurance payments and earnest money deposits.

13. **Fixed Rate Mortgage**—A mortgage in which the interest rate remains constant and fixed throughout the life of the loan.

14. **Loan-to-value**—The ratio between the amount of the mortgage loan and the appraised value of the property.

15. **Market Value**—The price that a property could possibly bring in the marketplace.

16. **Origination Fee**—A fee charged by a lender for processing a loan application. This is usually computed as a percentage of the loan and is used by some lenders as another name for "points."

17. **PITI**—An acronym referring to principal, interest, taxes, and insurance

18. **Points**—Prepaid interest charged by the lender. One point is equal to 1 percent of the loan amount (on a $200,000 mortgage, 1 point = $2000).

19. **Private Mortgage Insurance (PMI)**—Insurance that protects lenders against loss if a borrower defaults. This is required when the loan-to-value ratio is greater than 80 percent. The PMI payment may be tax deductible, depending on the situation, and is usually added to the monthly mortgage payment.

20. **Underwriting**—The decision-making process of granting a loan to a potential homebuyer.

# Chapter 22

---

*Most people give up just when they're about to achieve success. They quit on the one-yard line. They give up at the last minute of the game, one foot from a winning touchdown.*
Ross Perrot, American billionaire

**Keys to Having a Successful Home-Buying Experience**

**1)    Separate the Emotion from the Buying Experience -**

Buying a home can be a very emotional experience, but it does not *have* to be. When you purchase a home, you've decided to make a good financial choice. And that is what it simply is, a choice. The choice to purchase your very own home should not steal your peace or wipe you out. I've seen home seekers lose their minds as they went through the process. That's another reason why I indicated earlier that there is no such thing as "this is the only house for me." That is simply not true. Desiring to purchase a home you like is a healthy attitude; however, when this decision drives you to the point of anxiety, you may want to go back to step number one. Pray! I've heard, "I fell in love with that house" from new home buyers. Well let me clear something up for you. Never, ever fall in love with something that cannot love you back! The reasons you are buying your home must be separated from the process of buying your home.

**2)    Be Realistic about Your Expectations**

Your payment is directly proportionate to the size, location, and features of your home. Please don't be one of those who has caviar taste with a tuna fish budget. If you are interested in paying $400 a month, then keep in mind that you will receive a $400-a-month home. It's important for you to stick to your budget; however, understand that your payment requirements will have a direct impact on what you will get. There are certain aspects of your payment that you cannot control, and numbers do not lie. Don't despair, though, that you don't get everything you want. Remember, this may not be the only home you purchase; buying a less expensive home initially may be a good strategy.

### 3)  Protect Your Confidence and Have Enthusiasm

Hopefully you've gotten some good information from this book. You'll also get more good information at your eight-hour home buying class if you haven't already taken it. Now it would be unwise to go and talk to others who don't even have a home to get their opinions about buying a home. Have you ever noticed that everyone has an opinion *even* if they don't know the subject too well? Protect the information that you have learned. Don't let anyone steal your knowledge. You hired your mortgage loan officer and realtor to help you get all the information you need for a successful transaction. Try not to second-guess their professional advice by talking to a lot of people that don't know about your profile and the mortgage loan that you are seeking. Have confidence and enthusiasm as you pursue this worthy goal. Ralph Waldo Emerson said, "Enthusiasm is one of the most powerful engines of success. When you do a thing, do it with all your might. Put your whole soul into it. Stamp it with your own personality. Be active, be energetic, be enthusiastic and faithful, and you will accomplish your objective. Nothing great was ever achieved without enthusiasm."

### 4)  Don't Give Up!—Have Patience with the Process.

Author Tawni O'dell said, "Never give up on your dream…Perseverance is all important; if you don't have the desire and the belief in yourself to keep trying after you've been told you should quit, you'll never make it."

The essence of who you are is what you do and not what you say. And if what you say is not backed up with what you do, then the bottom line is that you are not committed. I often speak about my list of one hundred things I want to do. On that list, I've always included jumping out of a plane. Now, just because it was on my list, did that make me committed? The answer is no; I simply wrote it down but had not moved toward that goal. Several years later, my very good friend asked me if I was interested in going skydiving. I accepted the challenge, but still I wasn't committed. I really wasn't committed until I actually jumped (more accurately was pushed) from the ledge of the plane and went crashing toward the earth. This is when I was committed. Committed is actually making the jump. You see, I could no longer turn back; there was only one way to get to my goal. You must be committed to finishing your course. Hundreds of first-time homebuyers have attended our courses, but only a fraction of the attendees were committed to their goal. The essence of who you are is not what you say, but what you do.

Keeping this perseverance in mind, when a home seller says no, you say "next!" If one person tells you no, ask someone else. Remember, there are over 6 billion people on the planet! Someone, somewhere, sometime will say yes. Don't get stuck in your fear or resentment. Move on to the next person, home, or contract offer. It is a numbers game. Someone is waiting to say yes.

### 5)   Put Everything in Perspective

Although we have discussed numerous benefits of buying a home, I want to make it clear that buying a home won't fill any void that you have in your life. I hear so many first-time homebuyers putting everything that they have into buying a home. I always tell homebuyers to have faith—not in buying a home, but in what the Word of God says. In other words, whether you are able to get the home right now or not, if you trust in the Lord, He will keep you in perfect peace regardless. Trust says that even if it doesn't happen, my position does not change. It says that my commitment is not tied to what happens. Faith doesn't change *what* you see. Faith changes *how* you see. Faith says, "Tough...my contract wasn't accepted. I know that all things work together for good to those who love God and are called according his purpose. Therefore, neither my position nor my attitude will change. What God has planned is for me. So, if by chance this is not the right time to buy a home, it's okay. Your success has nothing to do with your ability to buy a home. As quoted by Pastor John Cherry II, "True success is in the will of God. Success means to prosper in every godly endeavor"

"Be Anxious for nothing". I really understood what this meant when I purchased my first home. As I mentioned, many homeowners find themselves getting attached to the home of their choice. Well what you think is best for you, may turn out not to be. I was extremely excited about my first home purchase. Like others, I couldn't sleep thinking about the fact that I would have my own home, my first home. Well, after going through the arduous task of processing and finally getting my loan approved, the day of closing was at hand. As usual and customary my walk through ( to make sure the home was still in good shape) was scheduled for 1 hour or so prior to the closing. While I was in "my new condo" looking around, my Realtor received a call. On the other line was the listing agent explaining that the seller backed out of the deal. Think about that, 1 hour before CLOSING, the seller backed out of the deal. Well, of course I was very disappointed and bewildered concerning the news. My plans and homeownership aspirations were dissipating before my eyes and there was nothing I could do about it. As I leaned on the balcony rail pondering, I noticed a for sale sign in the yard below the condo I thought I was purchasing. Eventually I ended up purchasing the condo on the first floor that was a MUCH better condo, at a lower price and it also had a yard. Talking about being in the right place at the right time. The moral of this story is that during this process it important that you are a perceiver and not a judger. You never know why things are happening and it could be happening for your good.

# In Conclusion

The decision to buy a home is a serious decision that should be undertaken only with careful consideration. The rewards of taking this monumental step are far reaching. For many years, purchasing real estate has been considered an extremely profitable investment, and it is an achievement that offers a sense of pride, financial stability, and potential tax advantages.

Yes, there are certain responsibilities associated with owning a home. Landlords will often argue the benefits of renting, and for obvious reason. If you are renting, you're helping them make *their* mortgage payment.

The numbers are staggering if you look at it this way. If you are paying $1,000 per month for an apartment (more than likely your rent will increase 5% every year), then over the next five years you will pay your landlord $66,309. If you are currently renting a house, you may be paying much more than that each month. Either way, you gain no equity by shelling out this monthly housing expense and you certainly won't benefit when the property value goes up!

However, if you were to purchase your own home or condominium, you would be on your way toward building equity. By choosing a fixed-rate loan program, you can have the comfort of knowing that your monthly mortgage payment will never increase. And not only would your own home give you added space, your own backyard, and overall privacy—home stewardship would also give you some tax advantages. Depending on your tax bracket, owning a home is often less expensive than renting, after taxes. Interest payments on a mortgage below $1 million are tax deductible. Your tax consultant will be able to give you more feedback on the tax deductibility of mortgage interest.

If you are financially ready to buy, the time to do so is *now*! Why? Because home prices *and* mortgage interest rates are the lowest they have been in years. Low home values are surely not good for people selling homes, but they are great news for people wanting to buy a home.

Taking the step into home stewardship is one of the most important financial decisions a person will make, so there are many factors to consider. Literally hundreds of loan programs are available, and it is important to find the one that best fits your personal long-term goals. First and foremost, you must have a knowledgeable mortgage loan originator in your corner who is willing to take the time to understand your long- and short-term goals. The loan originator should also be a person of character who has your best interests at heart.

Once you have found a reputable mortgage loan originator that you feel comfortable working with, lay your goals out on the table because this will have a tremendous impact on choosing a loan program that meets your specific needs. One of the most important factors to consider is how long you wish to borrow the money. For example, if you know you will only be in the home for five years, it may not make sense to opt for a thirty-year loan program or pay points up front to secure a lower interest rate. You will not be in the home long enough to benefit from such an action. Your mortgage loan originator should be able to narrow down a selection of programs based on the information that you provide and present you with an easy-to-read spreadsheet that clearly defines viable options for your interest rate and amortization schedule, monthly payment, and any potential savings you may realize by using certain strategies. Moreover, a reputable loan originator will not hesitate to share this information with your tax consultant or financial planner so that you can get additional feedback on your options.

Home stewardship is a rewarding vehicle for building wealth and a strong financial future. The mortgage consultant that you choose should be there not only when your loan closes, but should also provide you with ongoing service to assist you in managing that debt over time.

The process may not be easy and the journey will be filled with peaks and valleys, which will include some sacrifice on your part (believe me…you will have to sacrifice), but if done correctly, owning your home can help create real wealth and security for you and your family for many years to come.

I wish you all the best in your home stewardship quest.

Add more Derick W. Hungerford books to your collection…

**"The Mind of a Prosperous Homeowner"**

Review the contents of the "The Mind of a Prosperous Home Owner on the next page"

# The Mind of a Prosperous Homeowner

# Residential Mortgage Corporation

**Residential Mortgage Corporation** (RMC) is a licensed mortgage finance firm organized to provide mortgage loan products for home purchase, refinance, and investor financing.

RMC is committed to helping families and individuals achieve their dream of home ownership, asset accumulation, and wealth preservation. We are dedicated to serving and advising our community with sincerity, honesty, and integrity. We believe that today a mortgage loan is not as a mortgage loan once was, but instead a financial instrument that must be tied into the short- and long-term personal financial plan. We help our clients create a debt strategy that helps in building long-term wealth.

RMC is fast becoming a preferred lender for consumers and mortgage professionals across the country. Providing a host of diverse, flexible mortgage programs for customers with a variety of backgrounds and needs, RMC offers borrowers the strength and security of a forward-thinking mortgage firm dedicated to remaining an industry trendsetter.

Residential Mortgage Corporation has been a pillar in the metropolitan area for over a decade. RMC continues to help potential and current homeowners with their mortgage and financial needs. We believe that with today's volatility in the financial markets, it's vital to have honest, knowledgeable, and professional advisors to help guide the borrower through the market.

**The Residential Financial Advisory Team** was organized to further assist our clients needs. The advisory team is a resource dedicated to assisting borrowers in safely securing wealth by taking advantage of twenty-first century economic opportunities. We are a network of highly trained and forward-thinking financial advisors, money coaches, mortgage planners, and insurance specialists.

Residential Mortgage has been serving the public for over fifteen years.

# About the Author

Derick Hungerford is a Graduate of Hampton University and has more than seventeen years of experience in the mortgage industry. He has built an excellent reputation providing financial expertise for his clients and the community at large. He is a certified mortgage planning specialist (CMPS), which is a title held by only 5 percent of the mortgage professional population. As an accomplished corporate and financial strategist, his vision and expertise in mortgages has contributed to the increase of home ownership in the Washington Metropolitan Area.

Derick is an industry transformer who has created a unique system for managing home equity, called the Mortgage Empowerment Process. This process helps the client realize that a mortgage is a tool that can be used to ultimately achieve short- and long-term financial goals. Derick has a unique ability to help people grow fiscally by introducing financial principles to empower them to make clear, profitable choices for the future.

Derick is an industry educator and an instructor at RMC University and is the chief editor and publisher of *The Strategic Homeowner,* a bimonthly magazine geared to helping homeowners manage their mortgage and home equity properly. Derick was a host of *The RMC Home and Wealth Show* on Heaven 1580 AM. from 2000 to 2007 and is currently a certified teacher at several of the area nonprofit housing agencies. He is a licensed mortgage consultant, certified mortgage advisor (CMA), certified Mortgage Planning Specialist™, real estate agent, certified housing counselor, and insurance agent. He holds memberships in the National Association of Mortgage Brokers, Prince George's County Association of Realtors, National Reverse Mortgage Lenders

Association, Maryland Association of Mortgage Brokers, National Association of Realtors, and Certified Residential Mortgage Advisors (CRMA). Derick has a BS in business management from Hampton University. He is a member of From the Heart Church Ministries (under the pastoral leadership of John A. Cherry II), where he serves in the financial stewardship ministry.

## Take the challenge

The 21-day homebuyer challenge was designed to help homebuyers get prepared and ready to purchase a home within 21 days. Each day you'll receive an email with daily instruction, educational material and encouragement. Because we will be with you for 21 consecutive days you can consider us your "personal mortgage coaches" during this time.

Go to 21DayHomebuyerchallenge.com
Start your **FREE** membership today!

Also, if you complete the <u>entire</u> 21 day challenge, you will be eligible for up to **$2000** in credit towards your closing cost.